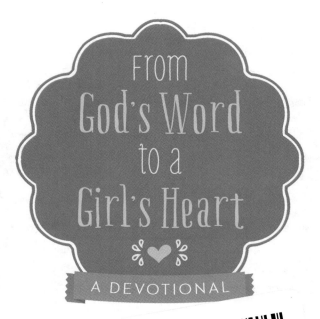

From
God's Word
to a
Girl's Heart

A DEVOTIONAL

Jani

SHILOH kidz

An Imprint of Barbour Publishing, Inc.

Published by Shiloh Kidz, an imprint of Barbour Publishing, Inc., 1810 Barbour Drive, Uhrichsville, Ohio 44683, www.shilohkidz.com

Our mission is to inspire the world with the life-changing message of the Bible.

Member of the
Evangelical Christian
Publishers Association

Printed in the United States of America.
000283 0420 SP

Great and Mighty Things for God!

There's no one on this planet who's just like you. No one has your same exact hair, your freckles, or your smile. No one has your laugh or your way of doing things. Before you say, "But I don't like my hair," or "I can't stand my freckles," just remember, God created you exactly like you are for a reason. The very God who created the universe, the One who decided that zebras needed stripes and cheetahs needed spots, decided the world needed one of you. Wow!

So what does God have planned for you? What's coming around the bend? Does He have great things for you to accomplish with your life? Sure He does! If He can use teeny-tiny bees to pollinate plants, if He can teach the beavers how to build dams in rivers, He can surely use you to do great and mighty things for Him.

The devotions you find in this little book will help you grow your relationship with your Daddy God while you're figuring out who you're going to be when you grow up. They will help you be the best you can be today so that you can be even stronger in your faith tomorrow. After all, if you're going to slay giants and speak to mountains, you're going to need to be strong from the inside out. So get ready! God is about to use His Word to speak to your heart. Ready, set...read!

YOU ARE LOVED

God has shown His love to us by sending His only Son into the world. God did this so we might have life through Christ. This is love! It is not that we loved God but that He loved us. For God sent His Son to pay for our sins with His own blood. Dear friends, if God loved us that much, then we should love each other. No person has ever seen God at any time. If we love each other, God lives in us. His love is made perfect in us.

1 JOHN 4:9–12

If you're like most girls, you dream of a happily-ever-after, a true fairy tale story. You try to imagine what it will be like to have Prince Charming show up on a white horse and sweep you off your feet, then carry you away to an amazing castle where you will live an adventurous life together. You picture yourself in a sparkling gown, dancing around the ballroom, while others say, "Wow, I wish I had *her* life!" It all sounds so dreamy, doesn't it? To be a princess in a fairy tale story seems almost too good to be true. Oh, but you *do* love dreaming, don't you? What little girl doesn't?

Here's the truth: You *are* loved by a Prince! Jesus is called the Prince of Peace, and He adores you. He thinks you're sweeter than a hot fudge sundae with a cherry on top. He thinks you're more beautiful than any model in a fashion magazine. And He would do anything for you—absolutely, positively anything!

Stop and think about that for a minute. The Savior of the world is your knight in shining armor! He's the One who adored you even before you were born. And He will go on loving you until you're old and gray.

Oh, sure, sure. . .it's hard to imagine you'll ever be an old woman. That seems a million light-years away. But you are on a journey to become an amazing woman of God, and it starts right here, right now. God can use you no matter how old you are or how many flaws you have. Instead of worrying about what a mess-up you are, just focus on how loved you are, how beautiful you are in His sight.

So no excuses! No waiting around for a prince on a white horse. He has already come. His name is Jesus, and He's ready to sweep you off your feet so that you can do amazing things together. Join Him for a lifetime of adventure. What are you waiting for, girl? Hop on that white horse, and let's get going!

YOU ARE UNIQUE

But you are a chosen group of people. You are the King's
religious leaders. You are a holy nation. You belong to God.
He has done this for you so you can tell others how God
has called you out of darkness into His great light.
1 PETER 2:9

You are unique. Stop and think about that for a moment. There's no one like you on planet Earth. Sure, others might have a similar hair color or skin tone, but there's no one just like you. It's not just your unique fingerprints that set you apart or your funny way of giggling. It's not just your freckles or your long legs. You are different in a thousand other ways too. Your heart, your love for others. . .it's all a part of God's clever and creative design when He came up with the idea of breathing life into you.

Maybe you're like Jenna, a girl who felt she was a little *too* unique. The youngest of three sisters, she felt so. . . different. Like an oddball. Her talents and abilities were different from those of her older sisters. Her curls were curlier. Her skin was frecklier. Even her personality was different. Her older sisters were fun-loving and outgoing. She was more withdrawn and shy. Her oldest sister could sing and play the piano. Jenna couldn't. Her middle sister was amazing at gymnastics. Jenna wasn't. She was just. . .Jenna.

Jenna's parents did their best to encourage her, but it did little good. Instead of celebrating her uniqueness, she just allowed it to make her sad. She didn't like being different. Only when she began to get older did Jenna start to see her differences as a good thing. She realized that God had placed special gifts inside of her that her sisters didn't have. She was really good at writing. And she loved to visit with older people in her neighborhood and listen to their stories about the good old days. She used her writing skills to help them write those stories down, which they enjoyed. It didn't take long for Jenna to realize that God had big things in store for her.

What about you? What's different about you? Are you celebrating those differences or wishing you were just like everyone else? Remember, God made you to be unique so that you could impact your world for Him. Instead of moaning and groaning about how others are prettier, smarter, or more talented, change your mind-set. It's time to enjoy your differences.

You Can Accomplish Many Goals

*"But you, take courage! Do not let your hands
be weak, for your work shall be rewarded."*
2 CHRONICLES 15:7 ESV

If you could see into the future, what do you think you would see? Wouldn't it be fun to pull back the curtain and see now what you will do then? (How exciting!) What kind of woman will you become? Will you accomplish great things? Will you travel to fun and exciting places?

If you're like most girls, you want to do big things with your life. Maybe you'll discover the cure for cancer. Perhaps you'll be a missionary, taking the Gospel message to tribes in third-world countries. Maybe you'll fly on a rocket ship to the moon. Or maybe you'll run for president one day. (Hey, it could happen!) The sky is the limit, girl! You can do great and mighty things for God.

No matter what you think you'll grow up to be, one thing is certain: you need to start setting goals now. No one reaches her goals if she doesn't set them, after all. The Bible says we're not supposed to worry about the future, but that doesn't mean we shouldn't plan for it. If you were about to take a trip, you would map out your journey. The same is true with your life.

Maybe you're an athlete. You play softball, or you're on the swim team. You don't start out by being the top pitcher or hitter. You get better over time. But what if you never practiced? Would you become a superstar? No way!

You'll go far if you get your body in shape and practice, practice, practice. The same is true with your spiritual life. Start by setting goals to "grow" your relationship with God. Maybe you should make it a goal to read your Bible every day. For sure, set a goal to pray each morning or night so that you're in tune with God. It's also a good idea to eat right and exercise and to stay on top of your school assignments. Goals will help you do that.

Get ready for the trip of a lifetime, girl. Big things are ahead. Let's start planning!

You've Settled the "Forever" Issue

"For God so loved the world that He gave His only Son. Whoever puts his trust in God's Son will not be lost but will have life that lasts forever."
JOHN 3:16

Have you ever stopped to think about the word *forever*? What comes to your mind when you hear that word? Sometimes it feels like a test is lasting forever. Or maybe you feel like the school year is lasting forever. Perhaps you get sick with a cold and it drags on and on. You feel like you'll never get to play with your friends again. You say things like, "I've been stuck in this house...forever!" No matter how long it seems, forever is a lot longer than all that. Forever is...well...forever!

There's a really cool word you'll find in the Bible. That word is *eternity*. The Bible says that when Christians pass away, they will spend eternity with Jesus. Eternity means there's no ending. Ever.

Stop to think about that. Whoa. When you go to the movie theater to see a movie, it has a beginning and an ending. When you go to school every morning, you know you'll eventually go home. When you drive to your grandparents' house, you know you won't stay forever (even though sometimes you wish you could). We don't experience eternity here on earth in the same way we will in heaven. We live temporary lives. Things start and things stop. Heaven is not like that. It starts. . .but it never stops. It just goes on and on and on.

Our minds can't figure out eternity, but God has already placed it in our hearts. Right now He's preparing us to live with Him forever in heaven. Think about that. If you're like most girls, you're fascinated by what's happening in front of you right here, right now. You're not thinking about what heaven will be like (or how long it will last). You're prepping for that next school project or trying out for the softball team, but you're not really focused on eternity.

God wants you to begin to think about eternity now. Why? Because you're going to spend it with Him. And since you have already asked Jesus to live in your heart (you have, haven't you?), then that journey has already begun. It's a journey you'll keep taking. . .forever. . .and ever. If you haven't prayed this prayer yet, today would be a great time to do so: "Father God, thank You for sending Your Son, Jesus, to die for me. I accept Him as my Lord and Savior. I make You King of my life and ask You to forgive all my sins. Thank You for giving me eternal life, Lord. Amen."

YOU HAVE PURPOSE

The Lord will finish the work He started for me.
O Lord, Your loving-kindness lasts forever.
Do not turn away from the works of Your hands.
PSALM 138:8

You have a purpose. There's a reason you were placed on planet Earth. You have a job to do that absolutely no one else can do. Yes, you!

Oh, sure, you have no idea what that job is. You think, *Me? I'm supposed to accomplish something big with my life?* Yes, you! God has huge plans for you.

To have "purpose" means there's a reason behind your actions. You're not just going through the motions. You're not just getting up in the morning, brushing your teeth, putting on your favorite jeans and T-shirt, and heading to school. You're motivated (you're excited!) because you know that God can use you to change other people's lives. Your testimony (the story of what Jesus has done in your heart) can make a difference in the lives of the kids around you.

Wow! When you think about it like that, don't you get excited? The God of the universe has a special purpose, a plan crafted just for you. No one else can accomplish it.

Sally didn't really understand God's purpose for her life until she went to school one day and found out that her best friend's mom was really sick with cancer. The family didn't have insurance, so Sally decided to start a fundraiser to help Mrs. Johnson out. With the help of her teachers and parents, she spread the word about the fundraiser. They arranged a big BBQ, and several singers and musicians offered to play and sing. Her teacher set up a special bank account for the family. Before long the whole community was involved. Together, they raised the funds to pay for Mrs. Johnson's surgery. In fact, they raised even more money than she ever dreamed, enough to cover all the bills.

God used Sally to impact the lives of the Johnson family and also the people in her community. It all started with caring. Because she cared. . .she acted. She did something. Through this experience, she discovered that her purpose in life was to love and care for people. As she grew older, her sense of purpose grew and grew. By the time she was an adult, Sally was working as a social worker, helping people in need.

What's your purpose? What's one reason God put you here? Are you a helper? A friend to the friendless? A hard worker? Ask the Lord to show you His purpose.

Your Body Is a Vessel

Do you not know that your body is a house of God where the Holy Spirit lives? God gave you His Holy Spirit. Now you belong to God. You do not belong to yourselves. God bought you with a great price. So honor God with your body. You belong to Him.

1 CORINTHIANS 6:19–20

God only gave you one body to live in. Just one. So it's important to take care of it and treat it with the TLC (tender loving care) it deserves. Sure, you want to eat burgers and fries. Yes, you love to swallow down a big helping of ice cream afterward, but sometimes it's a good idea to keep a closer eye on your diet so that you can stay healthy. Sure, you're not really worried about your health as much as, say, your grandparents are, but it's never too soon to start taking care of you.

If you're like most kids, you stay up too late, get up in a rush in the mornings, and can barely get your act together before school. You don't always eat a good breakfast or start off your day with prayer or Bible reading. Then you wonder why you have a lousy day, why you feel so crummy all day long. It's important to take care of you because (after all) you're the only you the world has!

Deena learned this the hard way. She tried to do too much. She got behind on her homework because her afternoons were spent playing softball, helping her mom with the baby, playing video games on the computer, and hanging out with friends. Instead of getting her work done, she spent her time on other things. Just before bed, she would reach for her school folder and try to rush through her homework, but she didn't always get it done. She would fall asleep with her folder in her hand, half-completed assignments in her lap.

Sometimes Deena would stay up really late working on school projects at the last minute. She would wake the following morning groggy and grumpy, then trudge off to school with her half-finished project. On those mornings she was too tired to eat breakfast, so her day got off to a rough start. Before long, she wasn't feeling well. She came down with a cold. Her head hurt. Everything felt off.

Can you relate to Deena? Do you ever feel completely overwhelmed? The reason your parents want you to get good sleep and eat healthy food is so that you can do your best work. If you don't take care of you, who will? Your body is a vessel, and God wants you to treat it with respect.

you can Be positive

*Think as Christ Jesus thought. Jesus has always been
as God is. But He did not hold to His rights as God.
He put aside everything that belonged to Him and
made Himself the same as a servant who is owned by
someone. He became human by being born as a man.*
PHILIPPIANS 2:5–7

Sometimes you get stuck. You can't seem to stop thinking
about that mean thing someone said to you. Your mind
replays her words over and over. She hurt your feelings and
you want to get even, but God says there's a better way. You
really can get over these feelings and move on.

There will always be negative voices trying to discour-
age you in this life. At school. At home. Even in your neighborhood. All around you, people argue and bicker. But you
don't have to be like that. You can be a light in a dark world,
a positive reflection of Jesus for others to see.

Caroline had a hard time with this. She loved hanging
out with the other girls who lived on her street. Talk about
popular! She was one of the group. Then, one day, her best
friend said something really mean about a new girl at school
named Brenna. She kept on saying rude things about
Brenna, and before long all the girls were gossiping about
her. They made up stories about her family. They criticized

how she dressed. They even made fun of the way she talked. And they decided, as a group, that they wouldn't have anything to do with her when they were at school.

Caroline didn't know what to do. She knew this was wrong. In her heart, she knew it. And she didn't want to join in the gossip sessions, but the girls made it hard. Every day when they got together they ended up talking about Brenna behind her back. When they saw her at school, they would walk right past her like she didn't exist.

Her friends' mistreatment of Brenna broke Caroline's heart, and she finally worked up the courage to take a stand. It was hard, but she told the other girls that she wouldn't keep hanging out with them if they were going to put Brenna down. Then she did the hardest thing of all—she sat with Brenna at lunch. Her friends were angry and started saying mean things to Caroline, but she decided to tune them out. She closed her ears to their negative, hateful words.

Over time, the girls eventually calmed down. By the end of the school year, they were all friends and Brenna was part of the group. And it all happened because Caroline decided to do the right thing.

Have you ever been in a situation like that? Maybe you've had to tune out negative words. It's hard, but God wants you to do the right thing, even if it's the toughest thing you've ever had to do.

You Have an Attitude of Gratitude

Let the teaching of Christ and His words keep on living in you. These make your lives rich and full of wisdom. Keep on teaching and helping each other. Sing the Songs of David and the church songs and the songs of heaven with hearts full of thanks to God.

COLOSSIANS 3:16

"I want what I want, and I want it now!" Remember that line from the movie *Willy Wonka*? Little Veruca was used to getting her way. She wasn't kidding with her demands, either. She stomped her foot and glared at her father as she screamed those demanding words. Her parents always seemed to give in to her (she always got what she wanted), but is that a good way to live?

Sure, getting your own way sounds like fun in the moment, but always getting what you want can turn you into a selfish, self-centered person. You don't want to be like that. You want to have an attitude of gratitude. You want to say to your parents, "Hey, thanks for providing for me. Thanks for giving me a home to live in and clothes to wear. I'm so grateful!" You want to say to your friends, "Thanks for being my friend." You want to say to your teacher, "Thanks for working so hard every day. I see all that you do, and I'm grateful."

When you have an attitude of gratitude, it spills over

onto other people and they become grateful too. Think about that. One person (you!) can affect the attitudes of many.

Here's an example: It's Saturday. Chore day. Mom has told you and your brothers that you have to clean your rooms and then help her tidy up the living room. After that, she needs your help in the yard, pulling weeds. You don't feel like doing any of those things. You wanted to spend the day playing with your friends or reading a good book.

You grumble and complain, but finally start to clean your room. As you do, the Lord whispers to your heart, "Change your attitude!" In that moment, in a flash, you realize how blessed you are to have a house to live in. You realize that your bedroom is your own personal sanctuary, and you're grateful to have it.

Suddenly you can't wait to get your room cleaned up. You can almost picture how great it's going to look. As you pick up toys and clothes, you start to sing a song, and before long you've got the place spick-and-span. Wow! You dust the furniture, and you even vacuum the floor and pick up the crumbs under the bed. In fact, you get so inspired that you decide to move the furniture around to give the room a fresh new look. Mom joins you to help with that, and at the end of the afternoon, your bedroom looks amazing. You're so excited by it all that you can hardly wait to start on the living room.

A change in attitude can change your outcome. Everything changes when you develop an attitude of gratitude.

you've Been Renewed

This is the reason we do not give up. Our human body is wearing out. But our spirits are getting stronger every day.
2 Corinthians 4:16

If you've ever studied prefixes and suffixes, you probably know what re- means. The prefix re- means "again." To be renewed means God can make you new *again*. This comes in really handy after mess-ups. Instead of throwing in the towel (giving up), you can pray and say, "Um, God? Remember that re- thing? Can I have one of those? I need a redo. I need a second chance."

God is a God of second chances. And third chances. And fourth chances. And so on. Whew! Doesn't it make you feel better to know that He doesn't expect you to get it perfect every time? You'll make mistakes, sure, but He's right there to say, "Get up! Try again!"

He's a re- story that should bring a smile to your face. Hallie had a little bit of a temper. Okay, she had a big temper. She didn't mean to do it, but many times she would snap at her mom and say mean, hurtful things. Even though she didn't mean to be disrespectful, it just kept happening. In fact, it happened so often that she found herself grounded from her friends, her favorite TV shows, and even video games. Ugh.

Hallie made up her mind that she wouldn't snap at Mom again. She made a promise in her heart: "Lord, I'm going to do my best. Please help me!" For a while, things went well. Then, when her mom stopped her in the middle of a video game to put away her clothes, it happened again. She got into an argument with her mother: "Not right now, Mom! I'm busy. Can't you see that?"

Oh no. The look on her mom's face told her everything she needed to know. She had hurt Mom. . .again. Hallie put the game controls down, got up from the sofa, and walked over to her mother. She put her arms around her waist and said, "I'm so sorry, Mom. I really am. I'll put my laundry away right now."

In that moment, as Hallie said, "I'm sorry," she realized she had learned her lesson. After all the chances Mom had given her, she'd finally learned how to do the right thing. Hopefully next time things would go better.

Maybe you can relate to Hallie. Your parents have given you lots of chances. Don't give up. You're making progress, whether you can see it or not. Choose to do the right thing.

YOU Are Not Afraid of Change

For if a man belongs to Christ, he is a new person.
The old life is gone. New life has begun.
2 CORINTHIANS 5:17

What if life was exactly the same day after day? What if you always wore the same clothes, ate the same food, talked to the same people, went to the same places? What if every conversation with your best friend was exactly the same as the conversation from yesterday? What if the lunch lady at school put chicken nuggets on your plate just like yesterday and the day before that. . .and the day before that? Wouldn't life be boring?

Thank goodness, life isn't boring! It's filled with changes, but that's part of what makes it exciting. Sometimes the changes seem overwhelming (or even scary), but you can count on God to see you through every one of them.

Here's an example of some of the changes you'll go through in life: Let's say you have friends in school one year and they move away the next. That's hard, right? But you eventually settle in with your new friends and enjoy your year. Let's say you have a teacher you love one year and then you move up a grade to a teacher who's not your favorite. That's okay. By the end of the year, she seems pretty nice. Here's another example: Let's say your family lives in a home you love but then moves to a new neighborhood where you don't know anyone. At first you're upset, but after a while you've made a bunch of new friends and you love your new place.

Change, change, change. Everything seems to be swirling around you like a swarm of bees buzzing in their hive. Change is hard, for sure, but never boring! And remember, God never changes. The Bible says He's the same yesterday, today, and forever. Even when everything around you is changing, you can count on Him to remain steady. So don't panic when changes come. God will hold your heart safely in place throughout it all.

Stop and think about the changes you've been through. What was the hardest one so far? How did you get through it? Was God faithful throughout that season of your life? Did He prove His faithfulness to you? Next time you go through a season of change, just remember what He did last time, how He remained the same. He will never leave you, even if everything around you is rushing out of control.

God Is Proud of You

Do your best to know that God is pleased with you.
Be as a workman who has nothing to be ashamed of.
Teach the words of truth in the right way.
2 TIMOTHY 2:15

Have you ever been in a musical production? Maybe your school class put on a show and your parents came to watch. Or maybe you were in a community theater production and your best friend sat in the audience while you performed. You got to put on a costume and go up on the big stage to sing, act, or dance. Afterward, the audience clapped and clapped, especially your best friend. She could hardly wait to tell you what a great job you'd done. And your mom! Could she be any prouder? All those hugs and kisses were over the top.

No doubt you loved the way it felt when people took the time to compliment or flatter you. It's an amazing thing, to have the praise and applause of people who think you're terrific at something. If you're like most girls, you soak it up like a dry sponge when it happens, and you learn how to bless others with that same kind of praise when they do something amazing. That's what being a "fan" is all about, offering applause to someone who's done a good job.

Did you know that God is your biggest fan? He's in the audience right now, clapping like crazy! He's so proud of you. For what, you ask? He's proud of you for holding in your temper when you could've lost it. He's proud of you for telling your friend about Jesus. He's proud that you cleaned your room when your mom asked you to. There are so many, many things He's proud of. He's whispering, "Attagirl!" when you please His heart.

Jesus is like a proud Papa. He looks down at you and says, "That's My girl!" Then He claps louder than anyone else in the audience, not to embarrass you, but just to remind you that you are loved. Even when you mess up, He's not upset. He just picks you up, brushes you off, and says, "It's okay! I love you anyway!"

Do you feel His love, even on the rough days? Do you realize how highly He thinks of you, even when you don't give your best performance? Today, tell God, "Thanks for loving me so much!" And while you're at it, let Him know that you are His biggest fan too. If anyone deserves the praise, He does!

You Are Not Conformed to This World

Do not act like the sinful people of the world. Let God change your life. First of all, let Him give you a new mind. Then you will know what God wants you to do. And the things you do will be good and pleasing and perfect.
ROMANS 12:2

This is a tricky one! You want to look like the other girls look. You want to dress like the other girls dress. You want to be good at the things other girls are good at. But the Bible says you're not supposed to be "conformed to" the world. That means you're not supposed to be like everyone else.

The truth is, a lot of people in this world think you should act like them. They are happy to be the leaders and expect others to follow them wherever they go. But look at their hearts. Are these people you should be following? Sure, they have cool clothes. Yes, they have the latest, greatest shoes. And sure, lots of people think these kids are popular and cool. But "popular" and "cool" aren't traits that impress God. He's definitely more interested in the heart than in outward appearance. (Not that there's anything wrong with cute clothes and cool shoes.)

Think about a glass jar sitting all alone on a shelf. It's

clear and empty. You pour colorful sand inside it and the sand takes on the shape of the jar. If it's a round jar, the sand looks round. If it's a bell-shaped jar, the sand looks bell-shaped. The sand conforms to the image of its container.

The same is true with you. You're like that sand, trying to figure out where to fit in. Instead of trying so hard to impress the kids around you, work hard to please God instead. This makes His heart very happy.

Think about the red letters in the Bible, the words of Jesus. Pay close attention to them. When He says things like, "Love your neighbor as yourself" (Mark 12:31 NIV), try to do what He says. When He says, "Do unto others as you would have others do unto you" (Matthew 7:12), try to do that too. Jesus wants you to be like Him. You can conform to His image if you're not spending all of your time trying to be like the other kids you know. And God loves when you want to be like Him. (What daddy wouldn't want his little girl to be just like him, after all?)

You Have a Place in the Body of Christ

There are many people who belong to Christ.
And yet, we are one body which is Christ's.
We are all different, but we depend on each other.
ROMANS 12:5

Have you ever tried to put together a puzzle that was missing one piece? You get all the way to the end and the picture isn't complete because one teeny-tiny piece is missing. You search everywhere for it, but it's lost forever. It really bugs you that you can't finish what you started. You had planned to frame this puzzle and put it on the wall for all to see. Now you can't do that. People would just say, "What happened to that one piece? Did you lose it or something?"

In some ways, you're like that puzzle piece. The Body of Christ (the Church) just wouldn't be the same if you weren't in it. You're an important part of the picture. Oh, sure, you don't always feel like people would notice if you weren't around, but they would. Things just wouldn't be the same without you. God put you here for a reason.

The Bible says that the Body of Christ (the Church) is one body. How is that possible? Millions of people around the globe are Christians, after all. Are we all supposed to look alike, dress alike, speak alike? No way! We're all completely different. But we all need to have the same beliefs.

We need to believe the Bible when it says that Jesus is the only way to get to heaven. We need to believe Jesus when He said that He is the way, the truth, and the life. And we have to put our trust in Him.

The Body of Christ is healthy and strong to the extent that believers love and get along with one another. So it's important to love and respect the other people you know who are Christians. They might not attend the same church you go to. They might sing different songs. But they love Jesus just like you do, which means they're family. And remember, they are all puzzle pieces, just like you. If even one of them went missing from the box, the picture just wouldn't be the same in the end. We need one another. So. . .that pesky boy at church who annoys you? Just remember, God put him in the family too!

Don't worry!

Do not worry. Learn to pray about everything.
Give thanks to God as you ask Him for what you need.
PHILIPPIANS 4:6

Oh boy. You've got a big test coming up, and you're about to panic. You try to study, but your thoughts are in a whirl. You can't concentrate. You decide to take a bubble bath and then climb into bed. A good night's sleep should do the trick. Only, you toss and turn in bed, worrying about how things will go. Will you blow it? If so, will it affect your grade? Ugh! Why can't you sleep? You get up out of bed and study, study, study, hoping you'll do a good job. But you're so tired in the morning that you can't think straight. If only you could have slept instead. Maybe then you would do better.

There are plenty of things to worry about in this life. Some grown-ups worry about paying the bills. Others worry about their health or their friendships. Some bosses worry about their companies. Some parents worry that their children will give up on God and walk away from their faith. Some kids worry that their parents will end up getting a divorce.

Here's the truth: God doesn't want you to worry...about

anything. He's got everything under control, even the stuff that seems impossible. That girl in your class who doesn't seem to like you very much? God's working on her heart. That test you're worrying about? God's got it under control.

Not everything will go perfectly in this life. But even when things go wrong, God still doesn't want you to fret. Some parents really do end up getting a divorce. Some people really do get sick. Some people get into fights with their friends and don't speak again. But even then, God can still take care of things if you just trust Him.

He wants you to give all of your worries to Him. What does that look like? It's like you gather them in a pile, wrap them in a cozy blanket, and lift them up to God. You take your hands off your problems and place them in His hands. He's able to fix the things you can't fix, and He's able to deal with all your worries and fears too.

Don't wait. Whatever you're worried about today, give it to God. Don't hang on to it. Loosen your grip. Release it. Imagine it's like a balloon, flying away in the wind. There! Doesn't it feel good to let go?

All Things

*I can do all things because
Christ gives me the strength.*
PHILIPPIANS 4:13

What an amazing Bible verse. We can get a lot more done if we put our trust in God, not ourselves. In fact, the Bible says we can do *all* things through Christ who gives us strength. Wow!

Think about a weightlifter reaching to pick up a heavy load. If he says, "I can do this!" then he probably can. But if he says, "Whoa! That looks way too heavy for me!" then he probably can't. He has to convince himself that the task is doable. Otherwise he'll fail before he even starts.

In some ways you're like that weightlifter. God has big things for you to do. If you're timid and afraid, if you're scared to try, then chances are very good that you will fail even before you start. (You'll talk yourself out of it before you even begin!) But if you have courage, if you trust Jesus to give you His strength, then you can do amazing things for Him. You just have to remember that He's the one with the strength, not you. You don't have to be superhuman to accomplish great things for God. You just have to trust that He can work through you, even when you're feeling weak.

Here's a good example: Kiki wasn't the best at memorizing. When her teacher gave her a big role in the school play, she had a l-o-t of lines to remember. At first she just said, "No, I can't do it! I'll never be able to remember all of those lines!" After reading through the script, she saw how fun the part would be. She also figured out a way to memorize the lines one by one. She recorded them on her mom's phone and listened to them over and over.

Before long, she was starring in the school play. And guess what? She didn't forget one line! Because she told herself, "It's okay—I can do this," she actually did it.

What about you? Do you struggle with your confidence? Do you find yourself saying, "No way! I'll never be able to do that!" much of the time, or are you an "I've got this!" kind of girl? What you say can greatly affect what you do, so watch your words. Give yourself an "attagirl" speech and you'll get a lot more done. God will work through you if you believe He can.

Your Words Matter

*"For it is by your words that you will not be guilty
and it is by your words that you will be guilty."*
MATTHEW 12:37

You didn't mean to say it. The careless words just slipped right out of your mouth. You criticized someone you care about and ended up hurting her feelings. Now she's upset, and you don't blame her! You wish you could take it back. You wish you'd never said something so mean in the first place. Why, oh why did you mess up like that, and how can you fix it? Will she ever speak to you again? (You wouldn't blame her if she didn't!)

The truth is, words matter. You can build people up with your words or tear them down. You can give someone confidence, or you can make them feel like they don't matter. The choice is up to you. Every time you open your mouth, you get to choose. Will you be kind to your sister or snap at her? Will you treat your mother with respect or say something rude?

It's time to look at the Word of God to see how Jesus feels about your words. Check out today's verse from Matthew. Jesus said, "For it is by your words that you will not be guilty and it is by your words that you will be guilty."

Obviously, the Lord takes your words very seriously. He says that those words will make you either guilty or not guilty. Ouch! Have you ever hurt someone with your words and then felt guilty afterward? It's not a fun feeling, is it?

If Jesus takes your words seriously, it's time you do too. Don't carelessly throw them around, like trash going into a dumpster. Words matter.

So how can you improve your words? Pray every day and ask God to guide your thoughts. Your thoughts become words, after all. If you guard your thoughts, you won't be as likely to blurt out something mean.

And ask the Lord how to bless people with your words. Practice sweet things you can say to others: "I really love your hair like that." "I'm so proud of you for getting a good grade on your test." "You did really great at softball try-outs." These are just a few of the things you can practice. Those kind words will come in handy. Keep them tucked away for the perfect time. You'll need them just when they matter most.

you Face Each mountain with courage

*"For sure, I tell you, a person may say to this mountain,
'Move from here into the sea.' And if he does not doubt,
but believes that what he says will be done, it will happen."*
MARK 11:23

If someone told you to move a mountain from one location to another, what would you say? No doubt you would stare at that person like he was cuckoo! How in the world would you move a mountain, anyway? Would you dig it up, one shovelful at a time, then walk it over to a different place? Or would you blast it all with a stick of dynamite and put it all together again in a different location? Just the idea of moving a mountain seems completely impossible. Still, God's Word says you *can* move mountains. What in the world do you think Jesus meant by that?

There are many "mountains" in our lives that need to be moved. Take fear, for instance. Sometimes you're so scared that you feel frozen in place. That big old mountain of fear has you convinced things will never get better. But you can look at that mountain and say, "Fear, be gone in Jesus' name!" Then, just like that, fear can vanish.

Maybe you're jealous. Your best friend got the part in the play that you wanted. Jealousy is like a big mountain standing between you. Look at it and say, "Jealousy, be gone in Jesus' name!" It will fade away in a moment if you really want it to.

Maybe you're mad. Your parents grounded you for talking back to them and you can't watch TV or play video games. You have to stay in your room while your sisters get to play. It doesn't seem fair. You sit in your room, but your temper is flaring. You want to kick the wall, but that would get you into even more trouble.

The truth is, anything negative can become a mountain in your life. And those mountains get in the way of the good things God has for you to do. So what mountains are you facing? Anger? Insecurity? Unforgiveness? These obstacles can vanish if you pray about them and then tell them to go. Speak the name of Jesus over them and then watch them disappear. "Poof! Be gone, mountain! I don't need you here anymore. I've got things to do, so you'd better get out of my way!"

you love god's creation

*The heavens are telling of the greatness of God and the
great open spaces above show the work of His hands.*
PSALM 19:1

Stop for a moment and think about creation. Not just the
people, but *all* of creation. Bright twinkling stars dancing
against a dark night sky. That curvy crescent moon, hanging there in space like an ornament. Mighty rushing rivers,
moving downstream in a hurry. Jagged mountains covered
in fluffy white snow. A beautiful golden sunset disappearing
into the western sky. Amazing!

This world is filled with beautiful things, all made by
God. Colorful cockatoos. Teensy-tiny butterflies peeking
out from their chrysalises. Newborn puppies with their eyes
tightly closed, snuggled together in their bed. Bright green
lizards changing color to brown when they slither onto the
fence. Massive elephants traveling across the African plain
with their babies following behind them. These are all re-
minders of just how creative and imaginative our God is.

Isn't it fun to think about all the creativity that went
into making the world around us? God could have settled
for a black-and-white world with no color, no pizzazz. He
could have chosen to make zebras without stripes. He could

have left the spots off the leopards. He could've skipped the leaves on the trees. He could have made kittens silent instead of giving them a "meow." He could have left the colors out of the rainbow or skipped the idea of making rainy days.

But He didn't! He chose to make it all just the way it is, colorful and original. Pizzazz, pizzazz, pizzazz! And think— He made you too. . .just the way you are. You are a part of this glorious creation, perfect just as He made you.

All of creation—from the tiny leapfrog to the brightest star—testifies to the greatness of God. If you ever begin to doubt that God exists, just look around you. The sun is shining overhead, as if to say, "He made me!" The puffy white clouds are hovering, as if to whisper, "He made us too!" Every created thing is a reminder that our creative God cares about the world around us. And if He cares about the world, surely He cares about you too. So what's holding you back? Join in with nature to sing the praises of our amazing Creator!

YOU ARE GIFTED

*"You are bad and you know how to give good things
to your children. How much more will your Father in
heaven give good things to those who ask Him?"*
MATTHEW 7:11

There are so many talented people in this world! Some
of the girls you know are probably terrific singers. They
could stand up on a stage and wow people with their singing abilities. Other girls are amazing dancers. You see them
in their pointe shoes and think, *How do they do that?* A lot
of girls are super-smart. They sail through school, making
top-notch grades. They can't wait to get to college and do
something big and important with their lives.

Isn't it fun to think that God gave certain gifts to certain people? He didn't mean for everyone to be an amazing
artist or to act on the stage. It wasn't in His plan for every
single person to be an Olympic athlete or to become president of the United States. He specifically chose gifts for
individuals so that they could shine brightly for Him.

Traci wasn't so sure about that. She could easily see
that her big sister was talented. Everybody talked about
how good she was at playing the flute. And her older
brother, the football star? He even got a write-up in the

local paper. The whole town was noticing his talents on the field. When it came to her, however? She couldn't see her own abilities. She just felt like a big loser compared to her brother and sister. It wasn't until her teacher began to compliment the stories that Traci was writing that she realized she had a special gift too. Why hadn't she thought about that before? God could use her stories to make people smile.

What gifts has God been developing in you lately? Are you a good student, one who makes terrific grades in school? Are you a gymnast? A musician? A painter? Can you write a story or put together a poem? Can you sing like a bird?

Whatever gifts God has placed inside you, you can be sure He will use them to reach others through you. Everyone of those gifts was meant to be used to spread the Gospel message. He has big things planned for you, so hang on, girl! And keep on developing those gifts. One day you're going to shine like a star. In fact, you're already twinkling now!

This Is a Test!

*My Christian brothers, you should be
happy when you have all kinds of tests.*
JAMES 1:2

Have you ever taken a really hard test, one you were worried you might not pass? Life is filled with tests, and not just the kind you take in school. There are friendship tests, trust tests, even medical tests. There are financial tests, athletic tests, even tests of courage. If you ask the grown-ups in your life, they will tell you there are marriage tests, job tests, and "Do we have enough money to pay the bills?" tests. Whew! The testing just never seems to end. Even older people have tests. Many are dealing with health tests, grief tests, and much more.

Get used to it, girl. Life is filled with tests. Will you pass every one? Maybe not. But here's some great news: even if you fail some of life's tests, God will give you plenty of opportunities to try again and again. He never gives up on you, even when you fail the first time. Or the second time. Or the third time. (He never gives up on you, period.)

Picture this: You're trying out for the swim team. You have to swim the butterfly stroke from one end of the pool to the other in a certain amount of time to make the team.

You try but fall short. You don't quite make it in time. At first you're really disappointed, but you don't give up. You keep practicing, and the next year you try again. This time your speed is much better because you've been working so hard to get ready. This time you make the team and you know it's just because you practiced so hard.

A couple of years later you're winning medals in the butterfly stroke because you've poured your heart and soul into it. Now you have even bigger goals. You can see yourself learning new techniques, going even faster. You've passed the "I won't give up" test, and it shows.

That's how God wants you to get past the hard tests—just keep trying. Just keep going. Don't get discouraged when someone else does a better job than you. (There will always be people who can run faster, jump higher, or do better on the balance beam.) You just be the best you can be and watch as God grows you into a stronger person, one who comes through her tests with flying colors.

Make Each Other Strong

*So comfort each other and make each
other strong as you are already doing.*
1 THESSALONIANS 5:11

The Bible says we are supposed to make each other strong. What does that mean? Are you responsible for your friend's exercise routine? Is it your job to make sure she eats healthy foods and takes care of herself? Not at all! This verse just means that we build each other up (make others strong) with our words. Jesus wants us to speak positive things over others and build their confidence.

It's not always like that with girls, is it? Not everyone is nice. Some are downright mean with their words. Why do you suppose so many girls like to cut others down? Is it to make themselves feel better, do you suppose?

What about you? Are you the type of girl who builds others up or chops them down? Are you the type who talks kindly about others behind their backs, or do you say mean things? It's important to build your friends up, no matter what.

Take the story of Gillian. She was good friends with Dahlia. They had been close since kindergarten, where they first sat next to each other. But the other popular girls made fun of Dahlia behind her back. They thought her hair was ugly. They didn't like her clothes. They thought she was too chubby and not as pretty as the other girls. The popular girls started telling Gillian how they really felt about Dahlia. They wanted her to stop hanging out with Dahlia and just be their friend instead. How do you think Gillian responded? Did she join in with the bullies and say mean things, or did she stick up for her friend?

Gillian stuck up for her friend! In fact, she told the mean girls that she wouldn't keep hanging out with them if they were going to cut her friend down. She didn't care what they thought. She just wanted to build Dahlia up and make her feel good about herself.

Want to know what happened? Before long, the mean girls stopped talking about Dahlia. In fact, Dahlia became their friend after they saw how Gillian stood up for her. Isn't it wonderful to know that Gillian built Dahlia up with her words, even though the other girls tried to stop her? That's real courage right there!

Who are you encouraging today? Who are you standing up for? Be like Gillian. Don't let the mean girls get away with cutting people down. You can show them, by your example, how to love as Jesus loved. When you do that, you'll make everyone stronger, even the not-so-nice girls.

you press on

*I do not say that I have received this or have already
become perfect. But I keep going on to make that
life my own as Christ Jesus made me His own.*
Philippians 3:12

Did you ever see the movie *Finding Nemo*? There's an ador-
able little fish named Dory who becomes friends with
Nemo. She's a little scatterbrained. Okay, she's *very* scatterbrained! That means she's super-duper forgetful. Dory
can't seem to remember anything from minute to minute.
In spite of that, she has a motto: "Just keep swimming! Just
keep swimming!" Whenever Dory gets lost or confused, she
sings those words aloud: "Just keep swimming! Just keep
swimming!"

Sometimes that's what you have to do in life. When
you're overwhelmed or you don't know what to do: "Just
keep swimming. Just keep swimming." When you're having
a hard time in school: "Just keep swimming! Just keep swimming!" When your brother is getting on your last nerve:
"Just keep swimming! Just keep swimming!" When nothing
around you seems to make sense: "Just keep swimming,
girl! Don't give up. Don't give in."

God wants you to keep going, even on days when you

don't feel like it. It's not always easy to keep going, especially if you're tired or confused. Maybe you don't feel like going to school today. Maybe you don't feel up to cleaning your room or doing your homework. Maybe you're not in the mood to help Mom with your little sister. Maybe you're exhausted and just want to climb into bed and sleep for a few hours. But the "just keep swimming" motto will give you the courage (and the energy) to get the job done, and that's the more important thing. Before long, you can look back on all you have accomplished and say, "Job well done, girl!"

Why do you suppose God cares so much about our persistence? Why does He want you to keep going, going, going, even when you don't feel like it? He doesn't want any of His kids to get discouraged and give up. The Bible says we need to *press* on. It takes energy to press. God never said it was going to be easy. He just said that He would go with you, every step of the way.

What's holding you up? Be like Dory. Look your problems in the eye and sing, "Just keep swimming! Just keep swimming!"

YOU ARE BLESSED TO BE YOU

For You made the parts inside me.
You put me together inside my mother.
PSALM 139:13

Have you ever stopped to praise God for making you…you? Girls often look at others and wish they could be like them. They say things like, "If only I had her body!" or "Wow, I would love to have cute clothes like hers." Comments like, "Wow, her hair is so much nicer than mine. I'd love to have curls," tumble from our lips. Instead of focusing on our unique design, we're jealous of others.

Take Lisa's story, for instance. She always felt cheated. All the other girls were pretty. She felt like a plain Jane in comparison. The other girls had talents. She felt like a hopeless nobody. While others were courageous and filled with energy, she just wanted to hide away from the crowd and read a book. Or two. Or twelve. Even in the stories, she felt defeated. The characters in the novels had perfect lives, or so it seemed.

When Lisa finally realized that God had created her in His image, she stopped comparing herself to others and asked Him to spotlight areas of her life where she could grow and develop. He did! Before long, she felt more content with her appearance, more grateful for her quirks (even the flaws), and more at peace with who—and how—she had been crafted by the Lord.

Can you relate to Lisa's issues? Maybe you don't feel lovely, inside or out. It's time to "get rid of your stinkin' thinkin' " (as your grandma would say) and change your attitude. How do you go about that? Here are a few ideas:

Take a day to write down the reasons you feel blessed to be you. Maybe your list would look something like this: "I'm blessed to be healthy. Thank You, God, for my family. I'm grateful for my parents. Father, thank You for giving me a place to live. I'm so thrilled to have a home/apartment. I'm blessed with good food to eat. I'm grateful my dad has a job. I'm thankful that You show up in the middle of my problems, Lord. Thank You for helping me overcome life's temptations. What a blessing to have the Lord on my side when I'm going through trials." Writing things down helps so much because it forces us to see the good, and there's a lot of good to be seen!

No one has a perfect life. Or a perfect body. No one is perfectly gifted or overly talented. Most of us are insecure, at best. But it's always a good idea to take the time to express gratitude for our uniqueness.

You Can Give Soft Answers

A gentle answer turns away anger,
but a sharp word causes anger.
PROVERBS 15:1

Naomi just couldn't seem to help herself. When her mom said, "Go clean your room!" she snapped back with an ugly comment. She didn't mean to (and boy, did she regret it), but sometimes she just couldn't seem to control her angry words. Her mom would respond, "Naomi, you know better than that." (And she did.) But sometimes her anger got the best of her and she boiled over like a teakettle.

What about you? Do you ever get angry and spout off? Are you like a volcano, about to erupt? What makes you mad? Your kid brother? A boy at school? Doing chores? Do you get snippy when you're tired or hungry? All of these things can trigger anger.

The Bible says that a gentle answer turns away anger. When you respond gently to someone, then everyone calms down. But when you knee-jerk and make a big angry deal out of everything, things can blow up in a hurry. Tempers flare. People get mad. Whew! The situation becomes a big mess.

Naomi knew just how big a mess could happen. If she

really let her temper flare, she would end up grounded. After a while she finally figured out how to get herself under control.

You can do that too, you know. Getting yourself under control might seem hard in the moment, but it is possible. It's not always easy to give a gentle answer, but here are some things you can do that will help: Don't respond immediately. Take a moment to release a slow breath. Count to five (in your head). Make sure your hands aren't formed into fists. Relax them. . .and relax yourself. God can use you to calm the whole situation if you'll just relax and respond kindly.

Of course, the very best solution is to give your anger to Him. Pray something like this: "Lord, I've had a hard time letting go of my anger. I'm so tired of blowing up at people. I don't like the way it feels. Please help me, God. Take my anger. I want to get rid of it, but I need Your help."

When you pray that prayer, if you mean it in your heart, God will start to take that anger away. Before you know it, you'll be calm, cool, and collected. Things won't bother you like they do now. What a wonderful way to live! A soft answer really can turn away anger.

You Take Pleasure in Life

*How can we give God enough thanks
for you for all the joy you give us?*
1 THESSALONIANS 3:9

Life is fun! There are so many adventures to be had, so many great things to do.

Oh, I know. . .you have to do your homework, go to school, do chores around the house, and so on. But there are joys to be found even in tasks like that. Don't believe it? Next time you have to clean your room, make a game of it. Set a timer for an hour then turn on some fun, upbeat music. Sing and dance as you work, work, work, and then look at how much you've done when the timer goes off.

Chances are good you'll amaze yourself at how much you got done when you turned your tasks into adventures. See how many tasks you can complete in a ten-minute period. (Turn it into a race!) Pretend you're in the Amazon rainforest, picking up snakes! Imagine you're canoeing in a river, surrounded by crocodiles. Picking up those dirty clothes is a lot more fun when you make it into a game.

Here are some other ways you can make those chores soar! Make a list of five chores you need to do. Start with the easiest and buzz through that one. Then do the next hardest, and so on. You'll get a lot done, and by the time you get to the hardest one, you'll already feel like you've accomplished a lot, which will give you the energy to get that last thing crossed off your list. See? Even chores can be fun.

God wants you to take pleasure in life. He hopes you will stop and smell the roses. He wants you to dance in the sunlight and stare up at the soft white clouds. He gets a kick out of watching you hold the remote control and act like it's a microphone as you sing along with your favorite songs. More than anything, He loves when you take the time to worship Him. Your praise brings your Daddy God great delight! (To Him, it's better than cake and ice cream!)

Think of one way you can take pleasure in life today. Do a good deed for someone else. Dance in the rain. Paint a picture. Tell your grandmother that you love her. Do something special to make this day count. You won't be sorry you did.

you can make great choices

Who is the man who fears the Lord?
He will teach him in the way he should choose.
PSALM 25:12

Imagine you've been walking down one road then all of a sudden the road splits. You now have two choices. You can go to either the right or the left. You're not sure what's down the road to the right. You're not sure what's down the road to the left. But you have to choose one or the other. How do you know which one to pick?

Life will give you many opportunities to make choices, and they won't always be easy. Should you choose this outfit or that outfit? Should you buy the sandals or the tennis shoes? Should you eat the mac and cheese or the PB&J? Should you be friends with this girl or that girl? Should you study Spanish or French? Should you go to this college or that college?

If you asked your parents what kinds of choices they have to make, they would probably say, "Choosing to go to work when I don't feel like it," or "Choosing to cook dinner when I'm exhausted," or "Choosing to pay the bills when I'd rather spend the money on a vacation." Life is filled with tough choices, no matter your age, that's for sure.

When it comes to choices, one is more important than all the others. It's a choice God hopes you will make when you're young (and stick with all of your life). You can choose to follow Jesus. You can choose to make Him the Lord of your life. You can choose to invite Him inside your heart and make Him the most important friend you'll ever have. If you'll make this choice—to follow Jesus—all the other choices you make in life will be much easier. Why? Because He will be right there to help you decide. He'll whisper in your ear, "Choose to be a friend to *this* girl. She really needs you." Or maybe He'll whisper, "Choose to go to *this* college because I have great things planned for you there."

Think about what you have planned over the next few days. What choices will you have to make? Before you make even one, pray and ask God for wisdom. He's happy to help you out. Your parents aren't the only ones who want you to make good choices. God does too!

you are worthy of love

We have come to know and believe the love
God has for us. God is love. If you live in love,
you live by the help of God and God lives in you.
1 JOHN 4:16

Keli had a little problem. Well, actually, it was a big problem. She didn't like the way she looked. And because she didn't like the way she looked, she decided other people probably wouldn't like it either. She said things like, "They probably think I'm ugly."

Scared that no one would want to be her friend, she started to pull away from the kids at school. She didn't even try to be friendly because she was convinced she was too ugly to fit in with the prettier girls. At night before bed, she would stare in the mirror and whisper the words, "Look at you! No one could ever love you." She was convinced she would never have friends, simply because of how she looked.

Then a girl at school reached out to Keli and started talking to her. Before long, they were laughing together and playing on the playground. With every sweet and kind thing this new friend said, Keli gained more confidence. Over time she began to see that her friend saw value in her and wasn't at all concerned about her looks. And the older she got, the more she realized she wasn't ugly at all. Sure, her teeth were a little crooked, but braces fixed that. And yes, her hair was frizzy, but it got better with a good haircut.

Here's the truth: all of God's kids are worthy of love. Love isn't something you earn by acting a certain way or looking a certain way. You don't have to be a beauty queen to earn love. God loves all of His kids because they are His. Think about that for a moment. He's your Daddy God, and you're His little girl.

And here's the best news of all—no matter how you feel about your looks, God thinks you're beautiful. You are created in His image, after all. When He looks at you, He says, "There's My girl! Isn't she beautiful?"

You are worthy of love because you are His. Never ever forget it. And don't let the girls around you forget it either. The next time a friend says, "I'm so ugly!" remind her that God created her in His image.

you Are one step closer today

God has again set a certain day for people to go into His rest. He says through David many years later as He had said before, "If you hear His voice today, do not let your hearts become hard."
HEBREWS 4:7

Have you ever watched a runner in a marathon? She has to be very careful to pace herself. If she tries to do the whole thing in a rush, she will end up collapsing! If she paces herself, she will probably make it to the finish line.

The same is true with many things in life—writing a paper for school, for instance. Let's say you want to get it done in one week's time. If you set your sights on getting it all done at once, you will get discouraged. But if you break it down into smaller chunks (just a bit of writing each day), it will come together more easily. So you set tiny goals, a paragraph or two at a time, no more.

No one understood this better than Renata. She wanted to run in a local marathon to raise money for breast cancer awareness, something her mother had suffered through. Not really much of a runner, Renata started small. She didn't push off her first run until "tomorrow." She started "today." She didn't feel like it but decided feelings had nothing to do with it.

60

First, she focused on making it around the block. Then she slowly "grew" her distance until she could run a 3k. By the time the race day came, she knew she could make it to the finish line because she had worked herself up to it. No, it wouldn't be easy. Yes, it would be doable. What made it possible? She'd paced herself. She hadn't tried to bite off huge chunks. Instead, she'd worked in tiny sections. Piecing those small bits together, she'd developed herself as a runner and become stronger and stronger.

Maybe you want to run a marathon. Or bike ten miles. Or try out for the church's Christmas play. Or sing in the choir. Maybe you're not quite there yet and need to make progress. Learn from Renata. Take baby steps, a few at a time. Work yourself up to where you need to be.

No matter where you are in your journey, you are definitely one step closer to your goal than you were yesterday. Even if you slipped and fell, you're one day closer. Don't look back. Keep your eye on the prize. You can do this, girl! One foot in front of the other. Keep moving. Start today so that you have no regrets tomorrow. Progress begins right now. Before long, you'll be running with ease, and you'll wonder why you ever doubted yourself!

your mind-set can change

Don't be selfish; don't try to impress others. Be humble, thinking of others as better than yourselves. Don't look out only for your own interests, but take an interest in others, too. You must have the same attitude that Christ Jesus had.

PHILIPPIANS 2:3–5 NLT

Has anyone ever accused you of being stubborn? Do you like to get your way? If so, then you're probably one of those girls who makes up her mind about something and nothing can change it.

Here's the good news: God wants to change your mind. He wants you to be more flexible. He wants you to consider the needs of others before yourself. He wants you to think like He thinks. He wants you to humble yourself and put their needs before your own. It's not always easy, but it's a better way to live.

Maybe you can relate. Think about your least favorite food. What is it? Brussels sprouts? Liver and onions? Salad? Maybe you've made up your mind that it's awful. Then your mom says, "Eat your brussels sprouts!" You sit at the table for half an hour arguing with her but finally take a bite. Hmm. They're not too bad. So you take another bite. Before long, your mind is changed. One bite changed everything.

That's how life is. You don't always have to get your way. You don't have to put yourself first. There will be many, many times when you can choose to put the wishes (or needs) of another person before your own.

Kari had a problem with this. There was a girl at her school named Bella whom she didn't like. No matter how hard this girl tried to be Kari's friend, Kari wouldn't have anything to do with her. Kari was just plain stubborn where Bella was concerned. She'd made up her mind: "I don't like that girl, and I never will."

Then one day she saw Bella in the bathroom crying. She overheard her talking to someone about her mom having cancer. In that moment, Kari felt awful for the way she had treated her. She realized how mean and selfish she had been. So she made up her mind to try to be nicer. Over time, Kari and Bella became good friends. And when Bella's mom was finally cancer-free, Kari was invited to the party to celebrate.

See how great it feels to lay down your stubbornness? See how wonderful it can be to put the needs of others above your own? Sure, it's not always easy, but it's worth it in the end.

you can find the good

Look for good and not sin, that you may live. Then the Lord God of All will be with you, just as you have said.

AMOS 5:14

Are you one of those girls who's always looking for the bad in people? Do you notice their flaws, mistakes, and mess-ups instead of the good things they do?

Lori was like that. After a school program she had a lot of not-so-nice things to say. "Man, Susie did a terrible job on her solo, didn't she? Some of the notes were flat, and she didn't have a lot of expression. Why did the music teacher give her that part, anyway? There are a lot of talented people who could've done better." After seeing her kid sister's ballet recital, she told her mom, "Brooke stinks at ballet. Why is she even taking lessons? It's a waste of your money."

Wow. Lori just couldn't seem to help herself. She had to make negative comments about everyone. Except herself, of course. She rarely noticed her own flaws, including the way she liked to gossip.

Maybe you know someone like Lori. They only seem to notice the bad stuff (or the mistakes others make), and they are happy to point it out. In fact, they seem to take great joy in commenting on the flaws of others. Sometimes these people are so busy focusing on others' mess-ups that they don't even see the problem spots in their own lives.

You don't have to be like that. If you look for the good, you will find it. Instead of criticizing others, you can say things like, "That was really brave of Susie to stand up there and sing a solo. I'm so proud of her! I'll bet she's going to get better and better as time goes on." Or you could say, "My little sister is getting better at ballet every day! I'll bet she's going to be amazing when she gets to be my age."

Don't you want people to look for the good in you? God does! Instead of pointing out your flaws, He looks at you with love and admiration in His eyes. Instead of saying, "What a mess-up she is!" He says, "Wow, look how hard she's trying. That's My girl!"

Just as God finds the good in you, you can find the good in others. Just look for it. And you can find something nice to say about their performances too. You don't have to exaggerate, but a kind word will go a long, long way in building confidence in someone who's just starting out.

you can get beyond the sadness

Show me loving-kindness, O Lord, for I am in trouble. My eyes, my soul and my body are becoming weak from being sad.
PSALM 31:9

It happened a long time ago. Someone you know died. Maybe a grandmother. Maybe a favorite teacher. Maybe a good friend. Or maybe your best friend moved away to a different state. It broke your heart. You've been sad for a really long time. Sometimes you wonder if you'll ever get over it or feel normal again. You wonder if happiness will ever return.

Megan knew what that felt like. She was super-close to her grandma. They went on trips together, played games, went to the mall. They were BFFs. When her grandmother got really sick, Megan prayed she would get well. She couldn't imagine losing the person who meant the most to her. Surely God wouldn't let that happen. . .would He?

She kept praying, but sadly, her grandmother passed away. Megan was really upset with God. He could have healed her grandmother. Why didn't He? Why would He allow such an amazing person to die?

After her grandmother's death, Megan didn't really feel like doing the normal things. She didn't enjoy being with her friends anymore. When people would say, "Hey, let's go to the movies," or "Want to hang out at the mall?" she turned them down. Nothing felt right without her grandmother. She couldn't stop that horrible sick feeling in the pit of her stomach, and her heart felt heavy all the time. Sometimes she wondered if she would ever feel right again.

Grieving after a death (or the loss of a good friend) is completely normal (and healthy). God doesn't expect you to pretend to feel happy all the time, especially when something terrible has happened or you've been through a shock. But He doesn't want you to be sad forever, either. Give Him your broken heart. Ask Him to heal it. Then trust that He will do it. He wants to see you smiling again, after all.

Why does God want your sad season to end? Because He has big things for you to do. If you're stuck in sadness, you won't be looking ahead at the future. Don't lose your hope. Don't give up on the good things that are coming. Yes, you've been through hard times, but that doesn't mean your best days are behind you. You have amazing things ahead.

your Glass is Half Full!

*Now the God Who helps you not to give up
and gives you strength will help you think so
you can please each other as Christ Jesus did.*
ROMANS 15:5

There's more than one way to see things. You can look at a glass that is half full of water and you can say, "Wow, someone drank half of that water! Why would they do that?" Or you can look at the very same glass and say, "Wow, there's still half a glass left for me! That's awesome!" It's all in how you look at it.

Some people are half-empty people. They're always grumbling and complaining about others. They are critical of others. Nothing anyone does for them is good enough. They love to grumble, grumble, grumble. These people are hard to be around, aren't they? And it's hard to keep them from rubbing off on you. (When you hang around grumpy people, you tend to be grumpy too!)

God doesn't want you to be like that. He wants you to be a glass-half-full kind of girl, bubbling over and spreading joy. When others are whining and complaining, you can be thankful and kind. When others are acting selfishly, you can be joyful and filled with gratitude. When others are criticizing, you can speak positive, encouraging words.

Cindy was a glass-half-full kind of girl. When her dad lost his job, everyone around her was sad. But Cindy had a different way of looking at it. She said, "Dad, maybe God has a much better job out there for you, one that pays more money and one that you will really love." Sure enough, a few days later her father was offered a job at a new company, one with better pay and shorter hours.

Cindy's glass-half-full attitude spilled over at school too. When everyone else was panicking over a big standardized test that was coming up, she just shrugged and said, "Why is everyone so worked up? Do the best you can. That's all that matters." When the big day came, some of the kids were over-the-top nervous. Because they were so upset, many did not do well on the test. But what about Cindy? She was relaxed. Chill. And guess what? Because she was calm, she did a great job on the test.

What problems are you facing today? How are you looking at them? Change your way of thinking. The glass isn't half empty. It's half full!

you Are no Longer in Bondage

*You have not received a spirit that makes you fearful slaves.
Instead, you received God's Spirit when he adopted you
as his own children. Now we call him, "Abba, Father."*
ROMANS 8:15 NLT

What does it mean to be trapped? Do you think of an animal in the forest, wandering into a trapper's snare? Or maybe you think of someone with their feet caught in quicksand. Being trapped means you can't go anywhere. You're stuck. There's no way out. It's a terrible feeling, a hopeless, sinking feeling.

Of course, not every "trapped" situation is that dramatic. Think about a hamster in a cage. He's got a decent life in there (and he loves his little wheel), but sometimes he looks outside of the cage and wonders what life would be like. . .out there. He dreams about the possibilities, but he'll never know for sure, because he's trapped. He's stuck.

Now think about a prisoner who's been behind bars for years. It's finally the day of his release. He gets to walk out of that prison and into the sunshine once again. Can you imagine how he feels as he steps out from behind the bars that once held him captive? No doubt the sun is so bright it nearly blinds him. But he doesn't care. He's just so happy

your Hope is in the Lord

*While praying to God our Father, we always remember
your work of faith and your acts of love and your hope
that never gives up in our Lord Jesus Christ.*

1 THESSALONIANS 1:3

Where is your hope? Where does it come from? Who or what do you put your hope and trust in?

Think about this for a moment. You flip the switch on the wall and the lights come on. You put your trust in electricity all the time. Same thing with the car. Your dad puts the key in the ignition, turns it, and—*vroom*—the car starts! You have this same kind of trust when you turn on the water. You're pretty sure water is going to come rushing off the faucet, right?

We put our trust in all sorts of things. If the weatherman says it's going to rain, we reach for our umbrellas. If advertisers tell us we'll love the latest, greatest smart phone, we have to have one. If we watch a commercial telling us about a new kind of candy, we have to try it because it looks so tasty.

But though we put our trust (or our hope) in a lot of things, God wants us to put our greatest hope in Him. But what does that look like?

Jordan almost lost her hope when her parents got divorced. Her mom cried all the time, and her dad didn't spend as much time with her as before. He was busy with his new family. The pain of losing him was so deep that she felt sick inside. Jordan wondered if her life would ever be normal again. Sometimes she just wanted to give up and cry all the time like Mom. But she didn't give up. She decided to trust God, no matter what.

Some time passed and Jordan's mom got better. She stopped crying. She got a new job. She started to smile more. Before long, Jordan's life was looking pretty normal again. No, things with her dad weren't perfect, but they did get better, as long as she kept putting her hope in the Lord.

It was a hard season, but Jordan learned a tough lesson: she had to put her trust in God, not just in her parents. That's a hard one, isn't it? We want to trust the adults in our lives (and we do), but our greatest hope should be in God. People (even adults) will let us down from time to time, but God will never let us down, no matter what.

your joy is contagious

We are writing this to you so our joy may be full.
1 JOHN 1:4

Have you ever had the flu? It's awful, isn't it? Worst of all, the flu is very contagious, so you have to be extra-careful not to share it with others. You can't hug anyone or even shake hands when you have the flu. You have to cover your mouth when you cough because you could spread germs all over the place and start an epidemic! And when you start sneezing. . .watch out! You might just spread it to everyone on the block!

Did you know that joy is a lot like the flu? It's *very* contagious. When you're bubbling over with joy, it will spill over onto everyone else around. That grumpy lady in the booth next to you at the restaurant? When she hears your giggles, she can't help but smile. That girl at school with the sour expression on her face? One look at the bright smile on your face and her whole day can change. That cranky little brother of yours? Let your joy spill over onto him and he'll be giggling with delight.

God wants your joy to be full. What does that mean? Think about a glass full of lemonade. You add ice and it spills over the top and runs down onto the countertop below. That's how full God wants you to be. He wants your joy to spill over so that others will catch it (like the flu). You won't have a mess to clean up. (Joy isn't sticky like lemonade.) You will have a lot of fun sharing your joy with others.

Candy's aunt Mary was like that. . .always joyful. No matter what she went through in life, she always seemed joyful. Her laughter made everyone else happy too. Even when Mary got really sick with cancer, she never lost her joy. After she lost her hair from the chemo, she wore silly hats to make others smile. On days when she felt sick, she would still crack jokes and give the nurses the giggles.

Aunt Mary chose to be joyful. She didn't always feel like it, but she made a decision in her heart to remain joyful no matter what she went through.

You can make that decision too. When you're having a bad day. . .choose joy. When someone makes fun of you or hurts your feelings. . .decide to be joyful anyway. When you're not feeling great, you can still choose joy. If Aunt Mary could do it, you can too!

Say these words to yourself: "Today, I choose joy!" Memorize them. Say them every time you're feeling down, then watch your day turn around!

YOU Are surrounded by Beautiful People

You are all a part of the body of Christ.
1 CORINTHIANS 12:27

When you look around you, what do you see? More important, *who* do you see? Other kids in your class? Your family members? The elderly woman who lives next door? Your kid brother? Do you see the lady delivering the mail or the man delivering packages? Can you see the woman jogging with her dog or the little boy bouncing his ball? Have you noticed the lady getting into her car? She seems to be in a hurry! And what's up with that silly expression on her face?

This world is filled with wacky, wonderful, unique people. They're tall, short, chubby, thin. . .and everything in between. Some have brown hair, some are blond, some have dark skin, some have light. Some love music, others love to read. Some enjoy spicy food, others not so much. The point is, no two people are exactly alike. (They're like snowflakes! You'll never find two of those that look just alike either.)

Each person on planet Earth is magnificently loved by his or her Creator. That's right! God adores them all! (Do you ever wonder how He keeps up with all of His kids? How does He remember all of their names, let alone their addresses?) He's the ultimate Dad, who loves all of His kids equally.

It doesn't matter where God's kids live, what color their skin happens to be, or what language they speak. The love of God knows no social barriers. It sees past any physical flaws, any human divisions.

Stop and think about that for a minute. It doesn't matter our age. It doesn't matter our skin color. It doesn't matter if we're tall, short, chubby, or thin—God loves each one of us equally. Whether we live in a fancy house or a tiny shack in a third-world country, every one of us is loved by God. And because He sees each of us as special and unique, He wants us to see others that way too.

Open your eyes, girl! There's a big, wide, beautiful world out there, filled with people you can learn from. Sure, most of them look different from you. They dress differently. They even eat different foods. But if you don't count any of that, you have a lot of things in common with all of them. You're brothers and sisters, after all!

YOU ARE SAFE IN HIS ARMS

The name of the Lord is a strong tower.
The man who does what is right runs into it and is safe.
PROVERBS 18:10

Have you ever thought about the word *safe*? In baseball, a player is safe if he reaches a base before someone on the other team catches the ball. Think about this: What if he came close but got scared and stopped before touching the base? Baseball wouldn't be much fun to watch if the runner gave up before he got to the base, would it? The whole game would be lost! The spectators would feel like they had wasted their money on a ticket. Before long the player would lose his place on the team if he kept giving up. (Who wants a giver-upper on their team, after all? Strong teams want in-it-to-win-it players!)

People who are in the game to win don't give up, even when they're feeling defeated on the inside. Think about that for a moment. You often face challenges. When you feel frightened, you may feel like quitting. When you "drop out" (give up), you feel like the game is over. Instead, you need to keep running. You might just make it to the base safe and sound if you don't quit.

Robin knew what it meant to drop out. After her best

friend moved away, she froze up. She didn't want to make new friends because it just seemed too hard. Everyone already had their own special friends anyway. Right? What was the point in trying? She just kept to herself and didn't socialize at all. While other kids were playing, she read books. While they had slumber parties, she watched TV shows. She played video games. She didn't really get to know people outside of her home's walls.

This seemed okay for a while, but after some time she got lonely. Really lonely. It took a while, but Robin finally got back in the swing of things. She conquered her fear and started to make new friends. Before long, she was enjoying life once again.

Life offers plenty of opportunities to feel scared. And we're wise to move with caution, especially if we've been injured in the past. But God wants us to break free and live safe in His arms!

YOU WON'T GIVE UP

Be happy in your hope. Do not give up when trouble comes. Do not let anything stop you from praying.
ROMANS 12:12

All Belinda ever wanted to do was sing. She practiced and practiced, day and night. No one worked as hard as she did at singing. She watched as her sisters, her friends, and her school peers auditioned for choirs, productions, and ensembles. . .and did well. They all got picked but Belinda never made it. Not ever. The rejection broke her heart, but she refused to give up. Deep down she knew she would sing one day, but the whole situation seemed so discouraging.

When she got to middle school, Belinda's mom paid for her to have voice lessons. The teacher saw a spark of potential in young Belinda, so she worked with her on tone, pitch, and confidence. Little by little, her voice improved. Belinda wasn't a natural, so she really had to work at it, but by her junior year she had landed a spot in the choir and was singing with more confidence. By the time she got to her senior year, she was singing solos. Her teacher gave her plenty of pats on the back, which boosted her confidence. By the end of her senior year, things were going so well that she decided to study music in college. Maybe she would become a music teacher so she could encourage other kids.

What about you? Are there special gifts you want to develop? Are you good at dancing? Singing? Acting? Playing an instrument? Do you excel at softball? Volleyball? Gymnastics? Tennis? The opportunities are endless, as long as you place your confidence in God and practice, practice, practice. You won't get there in one day. It might take years of working hard. But if you never give up, if you truly feel called to something, if you dedicate yourself, you will get better and better with time.

Think about this for a moment: Jesus Christ came from heaven to earth, knowing He would one day die on the cross for our sins. What if He had given up? What if He had decided, "This is just too hard. I'm not cut out for this"? Thank goodness He didn't give up. He gave His life so you could live forever in heaven one day. How wonderful to have a Savior who kept going, even when things felt impossible.

You Know How to Rest

*The man who goes into God's rest, rests from his
own work the same as God rested from His work.*
HEBREWS 4:10

You're a girl on the go! All day long you buzz from place to place—school, sports, play practice, birthday parties, and so on. You love your crazy-busy life. But sometimes, at the end of it all, you get tired. Really tired. You want to crawl under the covers and stay there. Sleep sounds so good!

Lyn knew what it was like to be on the go. Three days a week she had to be at school early for band practice. After school, she had softball practice. On the weekends, she had games. She was also super-active at her church and couldn't wait to compete in the annual Bible quiz. On top of all that, she had homework. Lots and lots of homework.

After a while, Lyn was too exhausted. She was cranky much of the time and doing a halfhearted job with her schoolwork. Something had to go. As much as she hated to do it, Lyn decided to stop softball for a season. It was a tough decision, but she didn't regret it. After all, she couldn't do everything all at once, could she?

Maybe you can relate to Lyn. Sometimes you're so worn out you wonder if you can keep going. When you wake up in the morning, you're still exhausted from all the things that you didn't get done the day before. God wants you to grow up strong and healthy. He doesn't want you so exhausted that you can't stay focused on what matters. But what can you do about that?

Maybe it's time to make a list of all the things you're trying to accomplish. See if there's anything you can mark off the list. Is everything absolutely necessary? If you get rid of even one or two things, you'll have more time for what really matters—family time, time with the Lord, time to read your Bible, and time to sleep.

Ah, sleep! Doesn't that sound good?

Your Heart Beats with His

*"I will give you a new heart and put a new spirit
in you; I will remove from you your heart of
stone and give you a heart of flesh."*
EZEKIEL 36:26 NIV

Have you ever listened to the sound of a heart beating? Maybe you were visiting your grandpa in the hospital and heard the *beep-beep-beep* of his heart coming through the machines. Or maybe your doctor let you listen to your own heartbeat through her stethoscope. There's something so soothing about the sound of a heart beating, isn't there?

Did you know that God gives you a new heart when you make Him Lord of your life? It's true! It's not a physical heart, not one the doctors can see on an X-ray. God gives you a new spiritual heart, and it beats in sync with His.

What does "in sync" mean? It means that your heart beats at the same time (and the same rate) as God's. Basically, it means that you feel what He feels, you care about what He cares about, you love people the way He loves people.

Maybe you're having a bit of a heart issue right now. Reba went through a struggle like that. She was doing well in her relationship with the Lord until her cousin died. After his death she just couldn't seem to care about much any-more. It was like her heart froze up. She lived her life in the usual way. No one really knew she was struggling. But Reba knew. After a while, people started noticing she wasn't herself.

Reba realized just how hard her heart had gotten and decided to ask God to soften it and make it more like His. At first nothing seemed to be happening, but little by little she began to feel more like herself again. It wasn't long before her heart was beating in sync with the Lord's once more.

Have you ever been through a time when your heart felt cold and hard like Reba's? Maybe you wondered if you would ever feel normal again. If you're still struggling with feeling that way, ask God to soften your heart. Tell Him that you want your heart to beat with His so that you can reach others with His love.

you can proclaim freedom

The Spirit of the Sovereign LORD is on me, because the LORD has anointed me to proclaim good news to the poor. He has sent me to bind up the brokenhearted, to proclaim freedom for the captives and release from darkness for the prisoners.
ISAIAH 61:1 NIV

Stefani overheard her parents talking about her uncle. She knew he was having struggles, but wasn't sure—until she heard her mom say it—that he was an alcoholic. At first Stefani wasn't even sure what that meant. He drank too much? He was sick? He might end up in the hospital if he wasn't careful? She didn't know.

Stefani worked up the courage to ask her mom what *alcoholic* meant. Her mother explained that Uncle Bob was addicted to alcohol. He couldn't seem to live without it. Stefani knew what it meant to be addicted. She was addicted to video games. And candy. And mom's spaghetti sauce. What was wrong with that?

Stefani listened carefully as her mother shared that Bob's addiction was ruining his life. He couldn't stop drinking even though he had tried. The alcohol was making him really sick. Stefani promised to pray for Uncle Bob. A few months later, after spending some time in a special hospital, he finally gave up alcohol once and for all. The smile returned to his face. He started spending more time with his family. Things got better once his addiction was broken.

People are addicted to all sorts of different things, but some people really struggle with the big stuff—drugs and alcohol. Others are addicted to lying or cheating. Addictions can seem overwhelming and scary, but there's good news in today's verse. God has anointed (called) you to proclaim freedom to the captives. That means you can speak life and truth to people who are addicted.

That friend in school, the one who lies all the time? You can share with her that Jesus can help her. Even people with serious addictions can turn their lives around, if people like you will take the time to share God's Word with them.

Just as Special

*Then the way you live will always honor and please
the Lord, and your lives will produce every kind
of good fruit. All the while, you will grow as you
learn to know God better and better.*
COLOSSIANS 1:10 NLT

It's happening again. You're at a family get-together and your cousin is there—the one who's practically perfect in every way. Everyone is telling her how pretty she is. They're complimenting her gorgeous curly hair. They're bragging on her good grades in school. They're carrying on about what a great job she did in the talent show.

There you sit, right next to her, and no one even seems to notice you're there. You try not to let it get to you, but after a while it does. It's not that you're jealous, exactly; it's just that you feel overlooked. Does anyone remember that you got good grades too? Do they notice you've grown since the last time they saw you? Do they see how blue your eyes are or how much longer your hair has gotten since they saw you last? Can they see that you're special too? Or do they even care?

Situations like these make you wonder if you'll ever measure up. They cause you to think you don't have as much value as the next person, especially the really beautiful ones. But God wants to remind you today that you're very valuable to Him. In fact, you're so valuable that He sent His Son, Jesus, to this earth to die for your sins. If you were the only person in the world—just you—Jesus still would have given up His life for you, to pay the price for you, His precious child.

Wow, that's amazing to think about, isn't it? God thinks everything about you is special. You're created in His image, after all. You're His kid, His precious daughter. He doesn't compare you with others or brag more on one than the other. He loves everyone the same.

Here's some good news: the way you handle yourself in situations where others are being flattered shows your loved ones a lot about your character. If you get angry or jealous, they'll be noticing you for all the wrong reasons. Just keep on being that lovely, precious girl you are, and remember. . .God adores you. So do the people around you, even if they get distracted from time to time.

you make a Difference

Know that the LORD has set apart his faithful
servant for himself; the LORD hears when I call to him.
PSALM 4:3 NIV

Laura didn't think that she had much to offer. She wasn't the best singer, so she couldn't join the choir at school. She wasn't a neat freak. In fact, she had trouble keeping her bedroom tidy. She felt "less than" the other girls around her, though she never would have said that aloud.

One cool thing about Laura: she really cared about her friends. She loved to make them feel better when they were down. She liked making cards and notes for people who were hurting or sick. She enjoyed treating friends to movies and dinner. And when a friend from school had to be hospitalized for several days, Laura helped set up meals for the family. During this season, people thanked her for her sacrifice. Only one problem—she didn't consider what she was doing a sacrifice at all. Didn't everyone do stuff like this? Why did people make such a big deal out of it? Was she really making a difference, as they seemed to think?

The answer is yes! Her little "act of service" was a huge deal to her friend and her friend's family. And though she didn't think of it as having much value, the act of "being there" was indeed very valuable.

Maybe you've walked a mile in Laura's shoes. You've felt like you didn't have much to offer. Think about what a difference the simple act of gathering meals made for that family. There are so many ways you can bless others, even if you don't feel exceptionally talented in the ways that draw attention. It's better to quietly love and care for someone than to make a big splash, anyway. You honor God in your quiet caring, and you bring a smile to the faces of those looking on. You're not demanding attention or asking for applause. You're simply doing what comes naturally, which is probably why it doesn't feel like a big deal to you.

Sweet girl, take heart! Whether you consider yourself gifted or not, you do make a difference in the lives of those around you. You really do. And you can continue to do so in the years to come. Ask the Lord to show you how to bless others when they need you most. In doing so, your talents will shine brighter than any star on the Hollywood Walk of Fame!

You Can Trade In Your Ashes for Beauty

He has sent me to provide for all those who grieve in Zion, to give them crowns instead of ashes, the oil of joy instead of tears of grief, and clothes of praise instead of a spirit of weakness. They will be called Oaks of Righteousness, the Plantings of the LORD, so that he might display his glory.
ISAIAH 61:3 GW

Not every day of your life has been a good day. If you're like most people (young and old), you've been through some tough times. Maybe one of your parents has lost a job. Maybe a grandparent or family friend has passed away. Maybe you've been through a terrible accident. These hard times can feel like piles of ashes. You wonder when things will be normal again.

Clair really struggled with this. After a house fire, she and her family had to move in with a relative. She had lost everything in the fire—her toys, her clothes, her shoes. . . everything. Sure, she had some new stuff now, but nothing was the same. Her bedroom was gone. Her favorite blanket was gone. Everything she'd known and loved was in a pile of ashes.

She tried not to let it get to her. People kept saying, "You're so blessed to be alive! Thank goodness you and your family made it out of the house." They were right, of course, but that still didn't fix what she was feeling inside. Mom and Dad were still there. Her brother was still there. The house was being rebuilt. But sometimes she wondered if anything would ever feel normal again.

One of the most amazing things about God is this: He can take the really terrible things you've been through (even the very worst things, like what Clair went through) and trade them in for beauty. All the sadness and hard times you've experienced? God will use them for His glory. So don't focus on all the things you've lost. Don't spend too many hours fretting over the tough stuff you've faced. Instead, trust God to give you beauty for ashes.

That's what Clair did. She decided to let God take her grief and her pain and mend her heart. Before long the new house was built and she had a brand-new bedroom and a new sense of purpose. No, things weren't the same. But neither was she. She was stronger, more peaceful, and had more compassion for others who were hurting. She allowed God to take her ashes and use them for His glory.

YOU ARE NEVER ALONE

"Be strong and courageous. Do not be afraid or terrified because of them, for the LORD your God goes with you; he will never leave you nor forsake you."
DEUTERONOMY 31:6 NIV

Sometimes you wonder why you feel so alone. Even in a crowded room, you don't always feel like you fit in. Everyone else is in groups, and they may not want to let you in. Or maybe they're willing to let you in but you're not comfortable, so you hold back. You stick to yourself out of fear. It's strange to feel lonely in a crowd, but it happens to many people.

Lydia didn't like the word *alone*. She did everything she could to fill her life with friends so she would never have to think about that awful word. She always stayed busy, busy, busy so she wouldn't have to be by herself. Why did this word *alone* bother her so much? Because when she was only in second grade, her father moved out. She could remember every detail of the day he left. It still broke her heart. So she filled the hole in her heart with schoolwork and friends. Anything to keep from feeling alone.

As she got a little older, Lydia discovered that her "aloneness" wasn't a bad thing. In fact, she started enjoying her quiet times. One day while reading her Bible, she read a verse that told her she was never truly alone, even when no people were around. The Bible promised that God would never leave her or forsake her. What an amazing promise to a sweet girl who'd been through such pain. Discovering this truth brought healing to her heart.

What about you? Are you filling the emptiness with activities? With people? With food? Are you like Lydia, doing all you can to avoid spending time by yourself? Does being alone make you nervous or uncomfortable? Ask God to heal your heart so that you can begin to understand that being by yourself isn't the same thing as being lonely.

Remember, nothing you do can cause God to run away from you. Today's scripture verse is 100 percent true: God won't leave you. He won't forsake you. He's not going to turn on His heels and run. So don't fear the quiet. Don't fret over the "alone" thing any longer. Enjoy the quiet and rest close to His heart.

You Seek Him First

But seek first the kingdom of God and his righteousness,
and all these things will be added to you.
MATTHEW 6:33 ESV

When you're going through a hard time and you need to talk to someone, who do you turn to first? Your mom? Your best friend? Your brother or sister? It's great to have someone to talk to (we all need people like this), but don't forget that God wants you to talk to Him too. Put Him first. Seek Him first. Instead of calling out, "Hey, Mom! Where are you? I need to talk!" say, "God, I know You're right here with me. Can we talk for a few minutes? There's some stuff I need to tell You."

No matter what time of day or night, God won't turn you away. He's so happy when you ask Him to meet with you. When you come to Him first, then all the other things in your life will fall into place. (That's a promise from today's Bible verse!)

Presley had a hard time with this one. She always wanted to share everything with her best friend, Anna. But after Anna moved away, she didn't really have another best friend to share things with. Not having a close friend to confide in really bugged her. She made other friends and started sharing with them, but she wondered if she would ever have that one special friend again.

Here's the truth: God wants to be that one special Friend. He wants to be the first One you come to with good news or bad. He wants to be the One who hears about your day—the ups, the downs, and the in-between parts. God longs to be your BFF.

Why do you suppose it matters so much to God that you want to hang out with Him? The Bible says that He created you (and all of humankind) for fellowship with Him. From the very beginning, He wanted to hang out with His kids. (Imagine if you were a parent and your kids never came to see you, even at Christmas or Thanksgiving. How awful would that feel?)

Go to God first. Make Him your best friend. Visit often. Arrive early. Stay late. Hang out with Him when you're having a hard day and celebrate with Him when you're having a happy day. Seek Him first and everything else in your life will be much, much better.

You Have Been Set Free from Fear

*There is no fear in love. But perfect love drives
out fear, because fear has to do with punishment.
The one who fears is not made perfect in love.*
1 JOHN 4:18 NIV

Maybe you've heard the expression "scaredy-cat." Maybe someone has even used that expression to describe you from time to time. You don't like being afraid, but it's not always easy to be brave. There are some scary situations out there, after all! Sometimes you want to pull the covers over your head and hide away. Your knees are knocking, your palms are sweating, and you can't seem to speak in complete sentences when you're terrified. How can you ever overcome your fears and live in peace?

The answer is found in today's Bible verse. There is no fear in love, and God, through His great love, has set us free from fear! "How does that work?" you ask. If you come to Him and say, "I'm afraid, Lord. Please help me!" He will. You can also speak directly to your fear. Stand courageously and say: "Fear, you have to leave me, in Jesus' name!" and—*poof!*—it disappears.

Of course, it's not always that easy. There will be occasions when you have a harder time getting past those feelings of fear and trembling, but God is right there, whispering, "You've got this!" in your ear. With His help, you will make it.

Hannah really struggled with fear late at night. She had always shared a bedroom with her older sister, but when her sister left for college, Hannah was alone in the room. She tried to act cool about it, but some nights she struggled to get to sleep because she was afraid of being alone. She tried everything—reading a book, playing video games before bed, even watching TV. But once the lights went off, she got scared all over again.

She finally told her mom what was going on, and they prayed together before bed at night. Her mom prayed that Hannah would be at peace and that fear would not keep her awake. Before long, she was sleeping like a baby.

What about you? What are you most afraid of? People? Nighttime? Taking tests? Singing in front of a crowd? It's time to kick that fear to the curb and live with courage. Be gone, fear! You have *no* place here!

your needs are met

And my God will supply every need of yours
according to his riches in glory in Christ Jesus.
PHILIPPIANS 4:19 ESV

Have you ever opened your refrigerator, stared inside at the hundreds of food items, and then declared, "There's nothing to eat"? It might sound like a silly example, but that's often how it is when we forget to be grateful for what we have. We don't always remember that God is supernaturally supplying our every need. We're loaded with good things—a home to live in, parents who love us, friends to share the load, a great school—and yet we feel like we're lacking. We want more.

Do you ever catch yourself wishing you had more, more, more? If you could have anything you wanted in the world (absolutely anything), what would you ask for? More toys? Money? A mansion for your family to live in?

Before you ask for anything new, take a look around you. What do you already have? Grab a pen and a piece of paper and begin to write down all that you see: your house, your bedroom, your favorite doll, your books, your clothes, your shoes, your pets, the food in your pantry.

Whew! It's getting to be a long list, isn't it? What if you

took the time to thank God for every single thing on that list? What if you said, "God, today I'm so grateful for my shoes. I know there are kids in this world who don't have any. I pray that you meet their needs and give them shoes to wear, Lord. Show me how I can help!"

See how that prayer changes your perspective? Instead of wishing for nicer, trendier shoes, you're suddenly focused on that little girl on the other side of the globe who doesn't have any at all.

Gratitude is a wonderful thing. It's a lovely reminder that you already have so, so much. What a generous heavenly Father, who gives His girls all they need.

YOU DELIGHT IN HIM

*Take delight in the LORD, and he will
give you the desires of your heart.*
PSALM 37:4 NIV

Have you ever had a friend who totally cracked you up? Maybe she always made you laugh, or she knew just what to say to make everyone smile. Those friends are great, aren't they? They bring great delight to all who know them.

Maybe when you were a little girl, you had a special doll that you adored. Every time you saw her you couldn't help but grin. She had a very special place in your heart, and being around her made you feel good. You delighted in her.

Lisa knew what it was like to be delighted by someone. For Christmas, her parents gave her a puppy, a gorgeous black lab she named Coco. He was the most playful little thing ever! He ran in circles, chasing his own tail. He barked at his reflection in the mirror. He loved to run and play, but mostly he loved curling up on the sofa next to Lisa. There, he would roll over onto his back and wait for his belly to be rubbed. Oh, what wonderful hours they spent, cuddling together and loving on each other.

Lisa adored that pup. They grew up together. When

she went off to college, she could hardly wait to come back to see him. The minute she walked in the door of the house, Coco ran right for her. They were best buds, even after all that time. Even though Coco got really old, he still never forgot his first love, Lisa. And she never forgot him either.

That's what it's like to delight in someone. You get that happy feeling in your heart whenever they're around, and you can't wipe the goofy grin off your face. It's almost magical.

Did you know that you bring delight to God? It's true. Imagine a father whose face lights up in a big smile every time his little girl walks into a room. That's how God feels about you. He sees you come through the door and gets that happy feeling in His heart. You don't have to perform any tricks for Him. He's not waiting for you to impress Him. He delights in you simply because you are His.

In the same way, your heart should be delighted every time you spend time with the Lord, praying or reading your Bible. Worshipping the Creator, reading His Word, listening to His still, small voice—all these things will delight your heart. What are you waiting for? Grab that Bible and watch the smile appear on your face!

YOU Are Perfectly Imperfect

All of us make a lot of mistakes. If someone doesn't make
any mistakes when he speaks, he would be perfect.
He would be able to control everything he does.

JAMES 3:2 GW

Do you ever look at your imperfections and sigh? Maybe you think your thighs are too chubby. Maybe you're not a fan of your straight hair. Or maybe you're embarrassed because you're the tallest (or shortest) girl in your class. You compare yourself to others, which is never a good idea. Oh, if only you looked perfect!

Everyone wants to be like Mary Poppins, "practically perfect in every way." But no one really is perfect, except Jesus! It's good to try hard, but in this lifetime you'll never reach a state of perfection. Even the best student doesn't know the answer to every question on every test. Even the prettiest girl has things about herself she'd like to change. Even the best gymnast falls off the beam once in a while. As long as you're human (and you always will be, at least in this life), you will have imperfections.

Imagine you actually achieved perfection one day. Everything you did was practically perfect in every way. Your attitude was perfect, your actions were perfect, you looked perfect. How hard would it be to keep that going, day after day after day? You would get exhausted trying.

God never intended for you to be perfect. Sure, He wants you to do your best, but as long as you're living on planet Earth you will experience mess-ups and mishaps. There will be things about yourself that make you unhappy. There will be tests you fail, people you hurt, and mistakes you make.

One day you'll get to heaven. There, everything will be perfect in every way, but until then you have to offer yourself grace. The next time you get a B instead of an A? Grace yourself. If you trip and fall, get back up and try again. And again. And again. If you don't like the reflection you see in the mirror, stop being so critical of yourself. You're beautiful because you're made in the image of God.

The key to overcoming imperfections is to just keep going. That's what the Lord would want you to do. No, you're not "practically perfect in every way," but you were created by a God who is. You are perfectly adored by an awesome God!

You've Got the Joy, Joy, Joy, Joy!

*"I have told you this so that my joy may be
in you and that your joy may be complete."*
JOHN 15:11 NIV

Juli was one of those girls who always bubbled over with joy. Her friends would say, "Wow, she's always smiling. What's up with that?" They started to wonder if she was faking it, pretending to be joyful when she really wasn't. (Some people do that, after all—they laugh to cover up the pain.)

Juli wasn't pretending. She wasn't faking it. She was really, truly joyful, from the inside out. Why? Because she learned a little secret: You can give your troubles to the Lord. You can rise above them. Once she figured that out, she had a lot to be joyful about.

In school, the kids would see her smiling and couldn't help but smile too. Her joy changed the atmosphere of the room. If you hung out with Juli, you couldn't help but smile...a lot. She just had a way of making everything better.

What about you? Are you like Juli? Would people say that you bubble over with joy? Do you change the atmosphere in any room you enter? Or do people say, "She's cranky...a lot!" It's not easy to be joyful all the time, but you can ask for a refill of joy.

Yes, it's true! Just like your parents go to the gas station and fill up the car with gas, you can ask for a refill of joy. Just pull up to the tank (Jesus!) and say, "I'm empty! Fill 'er up!" He will give you the joy you need to get through the day. It won't be a "fake it till you make it" kind of joy. It will be real, straight from God!

Why is joy so important? Because the Bible says that the joy of the Lord is your strength. Take away someone's joy, and you take away their strength. (No wonder you feel like a wimp sometimes! It's time for a refill of joy!)

How full is your joy-tank today? Get honest with God. You can say something like, "Lord, I'm just not feeling it today. I'm kind of down in the dumps instead of joyful. Could I have a refill, please?" In that very moment, as you share your heart with Him, He will fill you up to the tippy-top with His overflowing joy!

YOU ARE ON A LEARNING CURVE

*I pray that your love will overflow more
and more, and that you will keep on
growing in knowledge and understanding.*
PHILIPPIANS 1:9 NLT

Kelsi decided to try out for the softball team. She hadn't really spent much time playing (or practicing, for that matter). But she had a desire to play. So her parents bought her a ball, a couple of bats, and off she went to try out for the local team.

Her tryouts didn't go as well as she would have liked, but Kelsi was placed on a team. That first season she spent a lot of time on the bench. When she did make it onto the field, she wasn't as great at hitting the ball as she would have hoped. Still, she refused to give up. Little by little, she got better. Before long, the coach realized she had a great arm for pitching. By the time her third season came around, Kelsi was a star pitcher. The longer she played, the better she got. By the time she got to her senior year in high school, college scouts were coming to watch her play. She had amazing possibilities.

Maybe you're like Kelsi. There's something you really want to do, but you're not the best at it. You want to try out for the lead in the school play. You want to do gymnastics. You want to play the flute. But you're scared because you know you're not "there" yet. You're on a learning curve. (That means you still have a lot to learn.) Go ahead and get in the game. Put in the hours. Do the work. It might take a while, but you will get better and better as time goes on. You are loaded with potential. One day your hard work will pay off.

The same is true of your relationship with Jesus. You're going to make mistakes, even if you try hard. There will be days when you forget to pray. There will be other days when you lose your temper and sass your mother. There will be times when you realize you haven't read your Bible for a few days. In other words, you will mess up.

Just like Kelsi practiced to become a star pitcher, you can practice to make your spiritual walk stronger. Keep at it, even when you strike out. Before long you'll be stronger in your faith than you have ever been. You're really going places, girl!

You Rejoice in Bad Times

Be joyful in hope, patient in affliction, faithful in prayer.
ROMANS 12:12 NIV

It doesn't make any sense to rejoice in bad times, does it? Usually people celebrate when good stuff happens. They celebrate at weddings. Birthday parties. Graduations. Anniversaries. They don't usually throw themselves a party when they get sick or when Dad loses his job.

Here's a fun fact: The Bible says we are to praise God in every circumstance. First Thessalonians 5:18 (NLT) puts it this way: "Be thankful in all circumstances, for this is God's will for you who belong to Christ Jesus." Be thankful in *all* circumstances? Even when tragedies happen? Even when someone you love gets sick or has an accident? It seems impossible, but having this perspective really will help you get through the hard times.

Are you feeling down in the dumps? Praise the Lord! Feeling left out? Go on and praise Him anyway. Thank Him for the friends you haven't made yet. (They're coming!) Are you struggling to make it at school? Praise God and ask for His help. Be joyful and patient. Things will get better. Be faithful to pray. Don't give up.

Marissa learned this lesson from her grandfather. He

was diagnosed with lung disease when Marissa was just seven years old. Because of his struggles to breathe, he had to take an oxygen tank with him everywhere he went. Instead of being down in the dumps about it, he was all smiles. He would come rolling into the restaurant with it and proclaim, "The party can start now! I brought the air!" Everyone would laugh.

As he got older, her grandfather's condition got worse. But even when he had to go into the hospital, he was in good spirits. She couldn't believe her ears when he told her that he wanted his funeral to be a party.

"A party?" she asked.

"Well, sure," he answered. "I'm going to heaven, the finest place ever. Give me a going-away party no one will ever forget."

And that's just what the family did. When he passed away, there was a party atmosphere at his funeral. People told stories, sang his favorite songs, and shared about his passion for spreading joy.

Wow, what an inspiration. We all go through rough times, but keeping our joy is important. Remember, God will never leave your side. He's right there, patting you on the back and saying, "You've got this, kid! Just keep going! Don't give up!"

Your Life Is a Remarkable Story

Let the redeemed of the LORD tell their story—
those he redeemed from the hand of the foe.
PSALM 107:2 NIV

Once upon a time, in a land far, far away, there was a girl named _____ .
(Fill in the blank with your name.) She was a kind and godly girl who loved Jesus and loved her family. She lived a great life and had some wonderful friends. She trusted God, even when things didn't go her way. Because of her great love for Him, God decided to use her to do amazing things with her life. Before long she was _____

_____

_____ .

(Fill in the blank with something amazing you hope to do with your life one day.) Wow, did she ever shine for Jesus. Everywhere she went, people asked her why she seemed so joyful, so full of life. Her life was a remarkable story, one that people shared for generations to come.

What did you think about when you read all of that? Is your life really an amazing story, filled with twists and turns? If so, who is the author of your story? Is it you. . .or God? (Hint: Most of us would love to take the credit, but

God is the real author of our stories. It's always better to let the One who created you decide where the story is going. He's the best Author on the planet. He did write the world's bestselling book, after all.)

God loves when you share your testimony. That just means you tell others the story of all the things He's done in your life—like that time you were sick and He made you better. Or that time you were struggling to get along with your friend and He showed you how to forgive her and be friends again. Or that time you moved to a new school district and God gave you new friends. All of those moments are tiny chapters in your great big story. And just think, there are lots of chapters yet to come!

How will your story end? Only God knows, but you can be sure of one thing: He has exciting things in store for you. Keep walking with Him. Whenever you're in doubt, follow His lead. He already knows what the next chapter will look like. You don't know yet, but you can trust Him to write an amazing adventure ahead.

you can finish well

However, I consider my life worth nothing to me;
my only aim is to finish the race and complete
the task the Lord Jesus has given me—the task
of testifying to the good news of God's grace.
ACTS 20:24 NIV

Have you ever heard the phrase, "It's not how you start, it's how you finish"? What do you think that means? Is God really interested in how we end the race, not just how we start it?

Take a look at Maddy's story:

Maddy was nine years old when she decided she wanted to get a puppy. She begged her mom and dad for months. Every day she carried on and on about how desperately she needed and wanted a puppy. Her parents knew that a puppy was a lot of work, but Maddy promised she would take care of him. She would feed him, bathe him, take him for walks, and cuddle with him. She absolutely, positively promised to do all the right things. After talking it over, her parents agreed.

The family adopted Riley, a German Shepherd mix. Maddy was so excited she could barely stand it. At first she took good care of him. He was a sweet (but feisty) little pup, so tiny and cute. Then, as the weeks went by, Riley got bigger and bigger and bigger. Before long, he was huge! It was harder for Maddy to control him, so she stopped trying. She still fed him, but gone were the days of playing. Gone were the days of fun walks around the block. Gone were the days of chasing sticks.

Poor Riley began to act up. He chewed up a roll of toilet paper. He had accidents inside the house. Before long, Maddy was ready to give the dog to a new family. She didn't want him anymore. Her mom said, "Remember all of those promises you made? You said you would see this thing through to the end." Only, she didn't feel like it anymore. Didn't Mom understand that?

Sound familiar? Maddy started well, didn't she? But in the end, she didn't finish well. Despite her good intentions, she gave up. Thank goodness, her mom and dad saw what was happening and helped out. They took Riley to obedience training, and before long Riley and Maddy were doing great together again.

Starting well is great, but finishing well is even better. God has great things in store for you, and He wants you to complete the things you start.

YOU Are a Girl of Grace

But to each one of us grace has been
given as Christ apportioned it.
EPHESIANS 4:7 NIV

What do you think of when you hear the word *grace*? Some girls hear that and think it means "graceful." They say, "Well, that's not me. I trip over my own feet!" Grace isn't about our ability to move gracefully at all—not physically, anyway. It's about our ability to live in a gracious, merciful way.

Some people take the word *grace* and break it down like this: GRACE—God's Riches at Christ's Expense. To be filled with grace means that we've accepted the Lord's free gift, and at no cost to us. We're blessed, even when we don't deserve it. (Think about the last time your mom decided not to discipline you even when you deserved it. That's grace!)

Imagine you've been given a million dollars. You've done nothing to deserve it. You don't even really know the person who gave it to you, though you want to get to know her once she's given the gift. You're overwhelmed by the extreme generosity and goodness of this stranger and feel the need to repay her somehow, but she won't accept anything from you. All she wants is for you to stop by her house every now and again for a chat. You don't mind that one bit! In fact, you're more than happy to spend time with the one who cared enough to bless you.

Understanding God's grace is a bit like that. We can't figure out why the God of the universe would choose to show us such favor, since we're such mess-ups at times! And yet He did. He freely offered all He had so that we could enter into relationship with Him, and also so that we would have all we need in this life.

God's riches at Christ's expense. Jesus, God's only Son, gave His life on Calvary so that we could have everything we would ever need. But it doesn't stop there. That same grace flows out of us toward others we spend time with. God gave it freely, and we need to give it freely too!

How do we do that? When someone interrupts you while you're telling a story at the lunch table, extend grace kindly. When that one boy at school loses his temper, show grace patiently. Be willing to offer grace because God offered it to you!

Ah, grace. It truly is amazing, isn't it? You're a girl who recognizes the gift of grace and is grateful for it.

Your Light Shines Bright

*"In the same way, let your light shine before
others, that they may see your good deeds
and glorify your Father in heaven."*
MATTHEW 5:16 NIV

Admit it! There are days when you don't feel like shining
your light for Jesus. You don't want to talk about your
faith or get into any debates with people who believe differently from you. You just want to be left alone.

Katy knew what that felt like. After sharing with her
friends that she was a Jesus-girl and liked going to church,
they started making fun of her. At first she ignored their
teasing. She didn't let it bother her. But after a while it was
hard to ignore. They said mean things like, "Go on and trust
in your invisible God! We can't see Him!" Sometimes they
said, "What's the point in going to church, anyway? Only
losers go to church."

She tried to explain that Jesus lived in her heart, that
He wasn't a human being who could be seen, but they just
made fun of her even more. After a while, Katy just stopped
talking about her faith. She didn't mention it anymore. The
kids eventually stopped making fun of her, but she was
ashamed of herself for letting them get to her. She wanted

to start shining her light again but wasn't sure how.

Here's a fun truth: By responding in love to her friends, she was already shining her light. By not saying mean things back to them, she was sharing the love of God. By continuing to hold her head up and believe in Jesus, she was demonstrating faith.

Maybe you can relate to Katy. Maybe you have been made fun of for your faith. Don't give up. Don't fight back when people think you're crazy for believing in Jesus. If you make an argument out of it, things are only going to get worse. Just keep on loving them and treating them kindly. And don't forget to pray. Can you even imagine how your school would be changed if some of those "We don't believe in God" kids gave their hearts to Jesus? Wow! The whole school would find out and before long others would be giving their hearts to Jesus too.

Don't give up. Jesus loves every one of those kids (even the ones saying mean things) as much as He loves you. And never forget this: the Bible says that one day *every* knee will bow and *every* tongue will confess that Jesus is Lord. They will know the truth. . .in time. Until then, keep on loving them. Keep on shining your light.

You Are a World Changer

*With all your heart you must trust the LORD and
not your own judgment. Always let him lead you,
and he will clear the road for you to follow.*
PROVERBS 3:5–6 CEV

As a young woman, Heather dreamed of changing the world. She went on her first mission trip when she was only ten and couldn't believe how many amazing people she met while there. The adventure made her feel warm and fuzzy inside. She wanted to make a difference in the lives of all the people she met.

Sometimes she wondered what she would be when she grew up. Would she live in Africa, maybe sharing the love of Jesus with tribal natives? Would she work in a mission organization, translating the Bible into the languages of people who don't know the Lord yet? Or would she end up being a mom, spending her days changing diapers and washing baby bottles? If so, could God still use her to reach others with His Gospel message, or would she have to give up her idea of becoming a world changer?

Maybe you can relate to Heather's story. Maybe you think about making a difference in the world. You wonder what the future will hold. You can see yourself working with orphans in India or with sick people in Kenya. Oh, the places you'll go! You can hardly wait to get started.

Take a look at today's scripture. If you're really trusting God with your whole heart, if you're leaning on Him for every decision, then you have to believe that He's leading and guiding you at every given moment. Trusting God is a little bit like getting in the car with your parents. You're not sure where they're going...but they are. They have a destination all mapped out and will get you there.

The same is true with God. He will get you there, wherever *there* is. Maybe it will be on the other side of the world, or maybe He will plant you right here in your hometown. After all, you don't have to look beyond the view outside your own window to find people who need to hear the Gospel message. And you can make a difference in the lives of your friends, your neighbors, and the other kids in school.

Many people really are called by God to go across the globe to preach the Gospel. Maybe you're one of them. But while you're waiting—if you're waiting—don't look down on the little opportunities He's giving you right now. Those little things are actually a pretty big deal.

Your Relationships Can Be Healthy

*The sweet smell of incense can make you
feel good, but true friendship is better still.*
PROVERBS 27:9 CEV

Brianna loved her friends and would do just about anything for them. They all knew they could count on her. Some friends counted on her more than others. They took advantage of her. One of her friends, Tina, had a lot of issues. She was always asking to borrow stuff—clothes, shoes, even money. And she wasn't very good at returning things. In fact, she usually just kept the stuff for herself. After a while, she even asked Brianna to help her cheat on tests. No way was Brianna willing to do that. Still, Brianna felt stuck. She wanted out of the friendship, but she always wanted to be a good witness. What would Jesus do?

Maybe you have a friend like Tina. She's always asking you for stuff. You love her and would do just about anything for her, but it feels like you're being taken advantage of. Be careful! Your generosity could lead to an unhealthy relationship, and before long, you just might find that your so-called friend has drained you dry! Maybe this dreamy friendship is turning into a nightmare!

God wants you to be a good friend, but He doesn't

want people taking advantage of you. Sometimes the best sort of friend is the one who speaks truth in love, even when it's hard. Especially when it's hard. If you're hanging out with someone who's draining you, this might be the time to speak up, before things get even stickier!

Take a close look at your friendships. Make a list with all of your closest friends' names on it. Take a look at who's encouraging you and who's draining you. Godly relationships are based on love, true, but they're also based on Jesus' teachings. He didn't drain His friends. He encouraged them, loved them, taught them, built them up. Go to the Lord with your list and ask His opinion. Be honest with Him about how you feel. He will show you who to keep on the list and who to gently nudge to the side. Sometimes we have to do that, you know. . .ease our way out of relationships that aren't healthy.

Jesus loved others, but He loved the Father more. When you're walking in close relationship with your heavenly Father, you'll have wisdom to make the right decisions. So be a friend, but keep those friendships safe and healthy.

You've Laid Down Your Grumbling

Do everything without grumbling or arguing.
PHILIPPIANS 2:14 CEV

Courtney made herself a promise: "I won't grumble and complain for thirty days." It was a big promise, and she secretly wondered if she would be able to do it, but she was willing to try.

Courtney did pretty well the first day, but she did get a little upset with her sister for swiping one of her toys. She didn't make a big deal out of it, though. Things got a little trickier the next day when right when she was in the middle of playing a video game, her mom told her to turn it off and do her homework. She wanted to pull the usual, "Just let me finish this one game, Mom!" but didn't. Instead, she went into the kitchen, pulled out her pen and paper, and wrote the essay for tomorrow's class.

An hour later, Courtney's favorite show came on TV. She was just settling down to watch it when Mom said, "I need your help with the dishes."

"Right now?" Courtney asked. "I'm watching my show."

She pointed to the TV, but Mom just shrugged. "I've got to bathe the baby and your dad is on a business call. The dishes have to be done, and you're going to have to do them because I'm too busy. It won't hurt you to help in the kitchen, Courtney. You're a big girl now. You need to learn how to start accepting responsibility."

Courtney's temper started boiling, and before long she was in the kitchen having a complete meltdown. She slammed pots and pans around while shoving them into the dishwasher. A few minutes later her mother came in, scolded her, and then took over and finished the job. Later on, Courtney felt really bad about how she had acted. More than anything, she was ashamed. She had promised herself she wouldn't grumble and complain for thirty days, after all. Realizing she couldn't carry out her promise even two days made her feel sad.

Maybe you can relate to Courtney. You've tried to give up grumbling and complaining, but it's so hard. When something interrupts your plans, you don't like it. You lose your cool. God doesn't want you to lose your temper, though. He wants you to learn how to control yourself, even when no one is looking. Yes, it's going to be hard, but it will be worth it. Before long, you will have amazing self-control. God can help you if you ask Him to. So go ahead. . .ask!

YOU ARE GOING PLACES

*Practice these things, immerse yourself in
them, so that all may see your progress.*
1 TIMOTHY 4:15 ESV

Do you ever dream about what you'll do when you grow up? Maybe you daydream about becoming a marine biologist. You will move to the Bahamas and enjoy a life in the tropics, taking care of dolphins and whales.

Maybe you dream of becoming a famous movie star. You can see yourself on the big screen, acting and singing, starring in popular movies. People all over the world will know your name.

Or maybe you have your heart set on being an Olympic athlete. You will be the world's fastest swimmer or the most amazing gymnast. You can see it all now! The TV reporters will snap photos of you and splash them all over their news shows!

No matter what you have planned for yourself, you're going places. They might not be the places you think, but God will use you in amazing ways.

So what does it mean to "go places?" Will you travel the world—jetting from London to Paris to Istanbul? Will you travel by plane, by ship, or by car? Does "going places" mean you're going to be famous? Will people all over the world know your name? Will the paparazzi (reporters) follow you, snapping photos?

Here's a cool story about a man who "went places." His name was David Livingstone. He was a doctor from Scotland. David decided to become a missionary. He traveled to Africa many times on medical mission trips. In fact, he discovered parts of Africa that hadn't been explored before, including Victoria Falls. He was an amazing man of God.

Things didn't always go as planned for David. He faced sickness and even lost his wife, who died after a terrible illness. You might look at his life story and think, *Wow, that's not how I want my life to go at all*. But David Livingstone changed the world by spreading the Gospel (and by making many discoveries). He's well-known and well-loved because of his courage, his good heart, and his love for Jesus and the people of Africa.

"Going places" doesn't always look like you think. So don't be surprised if God takes you places you never dreamed. It might not be Africa, but He will surely surprise you with all the places you're going to go!

you love your peace and quiet

"Be still, and know that I am God. I will be exalted
among the nations, I will be exalted in the earth!"
PSALM 46:10 ESV

Gilly loved to play and hang out with her friends as much as anyone, but also loved her alone time. Some days she just wanted to close her door, curl up in bed with a good book, and read, read, read. Other days she would go outside and climb up on the trampoline, where she would lie really still and look at the puffy white clouds against the blue sky.

People always wanted to interrupt her quiet time. Just about the time she got settled, her kid sister would come along and start jumping on the trampoline. So she would go into the house, where her brother was playing his video games. . .loudly. She would ask him politely to turn down the volume, but he would not. Then they would get into an argument and Mom would come in and say, "Calm down, you two!" She would send Gilly to her room for arguing. In that quiet place, Gilly would have time to think about what had happened. She also decided to pray and ask God to help her not to have a bad attitude next time. A lot of cool things happened when she got alone with God to pray.

Did you know that God is thrilled when you want to

spend quiet time with Him? He thinks it's great when you read good books and gaze at the clouds, but He loves when you talk to Him too. There, in the quiet place, He can whisper to your heart.

What kinds of things will He whisper? Things like, "I love you!" "You're doing great!" or "I really love your heart for others."

To Gilly, He said, "Don't get so upset with your brother. Stay calm next time."

What is God saying to you right now? Is He whispering to your heart? Maybe it's time to get alone with Him to see what He has to say.

You Are Full to the Tippy-Top

*But those who obey God's word truly show how completely
they love him. That is how we know we are living in him.*
1 JOHN 2:5 NLT

You know that feeling you get after eating a wonderful dinner? You feel satisfied. Full. Happy. Content. You're not opening the pantry door, wondering what else you can find to eat. You've had the very thing you wanted, and it satisfied you. In fact, it was so yummy-for-your-tummy that you wonder if you can get up off the sofa for the rest of the evening! Ah! Why not just sit awhile and enjoy this full feeling?

That same I'm-so-full-I-could-pop feeling can be yours every day as you walk with Jesus. You don't have to hunger and thirst after other things. When you love Jesus, nothing else looks appealing but your relationship with Him. Why chase after things like popularity? Who cares about the latest fashions or expensive shoes? You know those things will leave you feeling empty anyway.

Natalie understood the word *empty*. She felt that way a lot. Her dad moved out when she was ten, and her mom had to work every day. So Natalie came home to an empty house after school. Her mom would rush in after a long day and they would eat a quick meal, then her mom would do some more work on her computer. Natalie felt pretty empty and alone.

When she turned eleven, a friend invited her to church, and she decided to give it a try. She found a lot of friends there, including several teachers she loved. At first she wasn't so sure if she thought God was real, but after seeing how great these people were and hearing how God had changed their lives, Natalie started to believe in the Jesus they were talking about. Before long, she gave her heart to the Lord. The emptiness was no longer an issue once her heart was filled with God's peace and with the love of her friends.

Think of a time in your life when you felt empty. It's not a very good feeling, is it? There's a way to stop feeling like that, and it's pretty simple: Don't look for other things to fill the empty spaces. Only look to Jesus. Turn to Him, and ask for a "fill-up" today. God will leave you with that fuller-than-after-Thanksgiving-dinner feeling when you ask Him to fill you up to the tippy-top.

You Are a Reflection of Christ

The Son is the radiance of God's glory and the exact represen-
tation of his being, sustaining all things by his powerful word.
After he had provided purification for sins, he sat down
at the right hand of the Majesty in heaven.
HEBREWS 1:3 NIV

Mirror, mirror, on the wall, who's the prettiest girl of all?
Mirror, mirror, on the wall, who's the smartest girl of all?

Mirror, mirror, on the wall, who's the most talented girl of all?

Are you one of those girls who likes to stare in the mirror? Do you carefully examine your eyes, your nose, your lips. . .even your freckles? Do you fix your hair different ways just to see how it will look? Do you imagine what you'll look like when you're grown up? Will you be a reflection of your mom? Your dad? Your grandma? Will you look like your older sister, perhaps? (She's really pretty. You wouldn't mind that!)

Whether you like your reflection or not, chances are pretty good you know what you're going to see when you look in the mirror. You see yourself all the time, after all. But what if, one day, you glanced in the mirror. . .and saw Jesus staring back at you. Would that completely shock you?

"Mirror, mirror, is that me? Whose reflection do I see?"

The Bible says that you—yes, *you*—are a reflection of Jesus Christ. When you love the unlovable, you're reflecting Him. When you feed the homeless or care for those less fortunate, you're a direct reflection of your Savior. When you talk to that girl no one else will talk to, you're reflecting Him. When you mind your parents the first time they tell you to do something, you're the spitting image of your heavenly Father.

"Mirror, mirror, now I see! Just like Jesus I want to be!"

God wants you to be like Him in so many ways—in your attitude, the way you speak to your mom, even the way you do your homework or class assignments. You can reflect Him in the way you treat your siblings, the way you take care of your bedroom, and even the way you care for your pets.

If you're ever wondering if you're reflecting Him, just ask the question, "What would Jesus do?" If you're doing things the way He would, then you are reflecting Him. No, you won't actually see His face in the mirror. But people will see His heart shining through you, and that's a very powerful thing.

Mirror, mirror, on the wall, make me like Jesus most of all!

your strength comes from Him

GOD, the Lord, is my strength; he makes my feet like the deer's; he makes me tread on my high places.
HABAKKUK 3:19 ESV

Have you heard of that old cartoon, *Popeye the Sailor*? Popeye was weak until he ate his spinach. Then—*bam*—muscles! Courage! Supernatural abilities! Wow. Talk about the perfect solution. And it all seemed so easy. We all need a can of spinach from time to time, don't we? Oh, if only it were that easy. (We would be eating spinach all day long, just to get stronger!)

Think about the last time you were scared. How did you get through it? Did you pray? Did you talk to someone you trust? How did you develop your spiritual muscles to see it through? Chances are pretty good a can of spinach wasn't involved.

Your strength comes from God. When you feel weak (and we all do from time to time), don't get anxious. Don't give up. Just trust in His strength. It might seem impossible to believe, but with God on your side you can fight giants. . .and win!

Abby wasn't so sure. She was tired of trying to stay strong for everyone else in the family. Since her older sister had to go to the hospital for cancer treatments, everyone seemed to be falling apart. After a while, she felt like she was falling apart too. It was just too much. Mom and Dad were gone most of the time. When they got home at night, they were exhausted and emotional. Everyone seemed so worried and upset, and not just about her sister's health. Mom was fretting over money. Dad was worried he might lose his job because he'd missed so many days. Nothing was the same anymore. They didn't have meals together. They barely saw one another, in fact. The whole ordeal was wearing everyone out.

It took a long time, but Abby's sister did recover. Her father didn't lose his job. Her mom stopped worrying. Abby was finally able to relax. Somehow God had given them all the strength to make it through that rough season.

The Bible is filled with examples of people who were given strength to make it through. Think of young David in the Bible. He took down Goliath with just a slingshot and one smooth stone! It was nothing short of a miracle. He didn't need spinach. He just needed faith to believe that God was strong enough to handle the situation.

The same is true with you! You don't have to depend on your own strength. In fact, God can do more when you take your hands off and let Him take control. So what giants are you facing today? Are there areas of your life that feel weak? Give those areas to God and watch Him do what only He is strong enough to do. Before long He'll be knocking down giants all over the place!

You Are Stronger Than Temptation

No temptation has overtaken you except what is common to mankind. And God is faithful; he will not let you be tempted beyond what you can bear. But when you are tempted, he will also provide a way out so that you can endure it.
1 CORINTHIANS 10:13 NIV

Temptation. Ugh! How we hate it. We're living our lives, doing just fine, and then—*bam*—temptation hits. We see it with our eyes and want it. We're sure we won't cave, but then we do. After giving in to the temptation, we feel guilty. We promise never to fall off the wagon again.

Allie understood this well when she decided to save her money to buy a new bike. She needed over a hundred dollars. No problem. She would save money from her allowance and make extra money doing chores around the house. She even earned extra money doing small chores for the lady next door.

Over time, Allie had nearly seventy dollars set aside for her new bike. Then, while shopping with her mom one day, she saw a video game that she couldn't live without. It cost fifty dollars. She knew if she bought it, her savings would go w-a-y down, but she couldn't stop thinking about that game.

So she bought it. Now she was down to twenty dollars. She kept doing chores and added about ten more dollars to her savings, bringing the amount back up to thirty dollars. But one day when she was at the store, she saw the cutest shoes ever. They were twenty-five dollars. She kept thinking about that bike, how she wanted to ride it with the wind in her hair. But those shoes were so tempting!

Maybe you've been tempted like Allie was. You've told yourself, *I won't do that,* or *I won't eat that,* only to cave. Afterward, you felt so defeated. Don't let it get you down for long! Here's the truth: temptations come and temptations go. They will always tug at us, urging us to do the wrong things. But today's scripture offers a promise that no temptation—no piece of chocolate cake, no relationship, no toys or shoes—will overtake us if we allow God to take control. The Lord will provide a way out, if we ask Him.

So ask Him! If you're facing a temptation right now, turn your eyes away from it. Repeat these words: "Make a better choice." With God's help, you can and will. And when you make mistakes (and you surely will), don't beat yourself up. Just brush off the dust, wipe the sugar off your lips, and get back to doing the right thing. God will meet you there.

You can master new skills

*A wise man will hear and increase in learning,
and a man of understanding will acquire wise counsel.*
PROVERBS 1:5 NASB

You're not afraid to try new things, especially new skills. Auditioning for a local play? Why not! Decorating cakes? Sure, we'll give it a try. Learning how to sew? Of course! These are fun skills to master. And who cares if we don't get it right? It's just fun to try.

Some girls don't like to try new things. They couldn't care less about learning to paint or dance or sing. What a shame! God gave us incredible imaginations and intended for them to be used, not just in our youth, but all of our lives. There are so many things you could be trying!

Margaret understood this better than most. As a little girl, she'd had a sense of adventure about her. Always ready to try new things, she acquired many artistic skills. But when she started middle school, she gave up on some of her skills. Then she went to her friend's house and saw a beautiful painting on the wall. One glimpse of the outdoor scene and she was hooked. The vibrant colors took her breath away. Looking at the picture made her want to pick up a brush and starting painting right away. She wanted to rush to the art supply store and buy a canvas and paints.

A trip to the local craft store was so much fun. With her mom's help, Margaret bought paints, brushes, and canvases. She took them home and got busy painting. Her parents were excited for her. And her kid brother liked her paintings so much that he asked her to paint something he could hang in his bedroom. Over a period of time, Margaret put together quite a collection. Best of all, the hours she spent painting gave her quiet time to spend with the Lord. She could pray and paint at the same time.

What skill have you secretly longed to master but have been afraid to try? Cake baking and decorating? Crocheting? Floral arranging? Why not sign up for a class? Or watch some online videos and then give it a shot. Interested in singing? Take some voice lessons or join a choir to further develop your skills. The point is, it's not too late. God can take your desires and put wings on them. You can master new skills and draw closer to your heavenly Father in the process.

you've got work to do

*A sluggard's appetite is never filled, but the
desires of the diligent are fully satisfied.*
PROVERBS 13:4 NIV

Hanging out in your pj's. Enjoying a fun movie. Eating chocolates. These are all fun, relaxing things to do. But some girls have a problem getting out of their "relaxed" mode and back into a "get the ball rolling again" state of mind. Admit it, girl! It's more fun to be lazy sometimes. But when you've been quiet and still, it's hard to get going again. (And let's face it—you can't spend your whole life sitting on the sofa!)

Andrea understood that. She worked so hard at school. And when she got home she had lots of chores. Finally it was time for Christmas break. She had a few weeks off from school to rest and celebrate the season. Andrea put on her pajamas and never wanted to take them off again. Sure, she knew the day was coming when she would have to go back to school. But hanging around on the sofa sounded like a lot more fun. Watching movies. Nibbling on sweets. Resting. Snoozing. And who could keep up with chores when you were that tired? Chores could wait.

And wait they did, until her mom had had enough.

Mom understood that Andrea needed rest, but she wasn't keen on the fact that Andrea's bedroom was flipped upside down and the sofa was covered in cookie crumbs. Andrea decided to get dressed and get to work. She put things in order. Oh, she moved slowly at first. Her body didn't seem to want to cooperate. Finally, she got her energy back...just in time to go back to school. Go figure.

Maybe you're like Andrea. You love those seasons of rest and wish they didn't have to end. God instructs us in His Word to take a Sabbath rest. In fact, He created the Sabbath so we wouldn't work too hard. But resting seasons aren't meant to go on forever. Remember, a "season" is just that: a season. It's not a "snooze on the sofa for three days" sort of thing. So enjoy your downtime, but understand that God is preparing you for the road ahead, the work ahead. He has big things planned for you, girl, and wants you to be in the best possible shape to enjoy it all.

Breaking out of rest mode won't be easy, but you can do it. Stand up. Stretch. Take a walk around the house. Then, slowly but surely, get busy!

You Are Bought at a Price

You were bought at a price.
Therefore honor God with your bodies.
1 Corinthians 6:20 niv

Imagine going to a fine art museum and seeing a valuable painting. It's about to be auctioned off and the opening bid is fifty thousand dollars. Wow! That's quite a work of art! It's worth far more than you might guess at first glance. As the crowd thins, you give it a closer look. Hmm. When you look at that so-called priceless piece, all you see is an ordinary painting. Maybe it's even a little odd looking. You can't figure out why it's worth so much. It's certainly not something you would hang on your living room wall, even if someone paid you to do it!

What gives the painting its value is the artist. His name is written on it. An ordinary painting is suddenly worth a fortune if Van Gogh's name is on it. Or Rembrandt. Or Renoir. These artists are very famous, so their names add value no matter what the painting looks like. The name means everything.

The same can be said of you, sweet girl! You are a priceless work of art. God's name is written on your heart. That alone gives you so much value. It makes you priceless, in fact. No one could bid high enough to purchase you because they couldn't pay the price. Only the Lord could do that, and He has already done it!

Think about that for a moment. You were bought at a price and are more valuable than rubies or diamonds, more precious than any rare jewel, and more costly than any painting, no matter how famous the painter might be. The Master Artist took the time to craft you just as you are, a rare beauty. (That will change how you view your reflection in the mirror, won't it?)

How amazing to think that the ultimate Creator wove you together in your mother's womb. What an intricate work of art! And He paid the price for you when He sent His Son to Calvary. You were worth so much to Jesus that He laid down His very life for you. Rarely would anyone pay a huge price for something they loved, even a valuable piece of art. But Jesus Himself paid the price for you. How valuable you are to Him! Others might not see it, but He does! And He never forgets that you are His personal design, created in His image.

How do you see yourself? Remember, you are more valuable than any Van Gogh painting. Don't ever forget it!

You Are Radiant

Arise, shine, for your light has come,
and the glory of the LORD has risen upon you.
Isaiah 60:1 ESV

Have you ever seen those paintings of Jesus that were done hundreds of years ago? Jesus is always portrayed with a heavenly glow around His head. The glow represented the glorious presence of God. Even older paintings of the disciples looked like that. They all had a heavenly glow. It meant they were set apart. In other words, they were sent to this earth to make a difference. And make a difference they did!

If you think about it, you have that same heavenly glow! It doesn't show up in pictures. You won't see it when you look in the mirror. But it's there, and it draws people to you just the same. The Bible says that you are a reflection of Christ, and He is the most radiant of all. You shimmer and shine for all the world to see, girl. Wow!

Sure, there are days when you feel like someone has taken a giant eraser and wiped that glow away. You just don't feel like shining. You'd rather be a grouch. But even on the worst of days you still do your best. You let your light shine, and it makes a difference in the lives of those around you.

Be careful when you're shining the light of Jesus not to point it straight into someone's eyes. It can be blinding! Make sure you share the love and light of Jesus in a way that doesn't hurt others.

Deborah learned this lesson the hard way. She wanted to be a good witness to her friends, so she made a point of quoting scriptures and lecturing them whenever they did bad things. Her heart was in the right place, but the way she was doing things was off track. People began to avoid her, calling her a Jesus freak or a religious nut. She annoyed them!

Instead of drawing people to the light, she found others running in the opposite direction whenever they saw her coming. Why? Because they saw her as judgmental and unkind. A more loving approach would have been better. She could have let her light shine but kept it out of their eyes.

What about you? Does your light shine brightly? Are you using it wisely? Are you reflecting God's love? Ask the Lord to show you the best possible way to reflect His light so that you can share His love with others in need.

you are careful who you listen to

*So be careful how you live. Don't live
like fools, but like those who are wise.*
EPHESIANS 5:15 NLT

A little song popular in kids' church years ago went something like this: *"Oh be careful little ears what you hear. Oh be careful little ears what you hear. For the Father up above is looking down in love. Oh be careful little ears what you hear."*

Why do you suppose God wants us to be careful with our ears? Are we supposed to wear earplugs to drown out the noise of life? Not exactly. We just need to guard what goes in because it will eventually come out.

Not sure what that means? Here's an example:

Some girls hang out with kids who use bad language. After a while they get used to it. It doesn't even bother them anymore. Then, without meaning to, they slip up and say a bad word. Oops! Why did that happen? Because they opened their ears to something bad.

Other girls spend time around people who gossip. The gossips are always spreading stories about others. The girls who are listening get used to hearing it, and before long they're gossiping too. They didn't mean for it to happen, but it did.

Some girls hang out with people who lie. They get so used to hearing their friends lie that they start doing it too.

Don't you see, sweet girl? That's how it works. If you open your ears to bad things, before long you'll get drawn in. You will become like those people. God wants you to be different. That means you don't lie, you don't gossip, and you don't use bad language. The best protection you have is to shut your ears to people who live like that.

Does that mean you can't be friends with people who do wrong things? Of course not. We all mess up. But don't spend a lot of time with people who break God's heart. Be a good witness to them. Let them learn from you. But don't pick up any of their bad habits. Stay strong in your faith.

Here are a few good ways to use your ears: Listen to a friend who's going through a hard time. Listen to your parents and teachers when they give you instructions. Listen to wonderful Christian music. Listen to the lessons you get at church. Listen to the sound of a bird singing outside your window. Listen to the wind as it blows through the trees. Most of all, listen for God's still, small voice. He wants to speak to your heart, you know.

You've Learned to Live a Balanced Life

He replied, "You of little faith, why are you so afraid?"
Then he got up and rebuked the winds and
the waves, and it was completely calm.
MATTHEW 8:26 NIV

What does it mean to be balanced? Think of a gymnast on a balance beam. She tries so hard to stay up there, but if she sways too far to the right or left, down she goes! A "balanced" person is centered. She spends more time on the beam and less on the ground. Can you even imagine what a tightrope walker would go through if she lost her balance? Eek!

Amy had a harder time than most with living in balance. She was like a pendulum, swinging back and forth. She was sweet and loving one day then snippy and snappy the next. She worked really hard one day then slacked off the next. She ate healthy foods one day then binged on junk food the next. She just couldn't figure out how to live a balanced life. Back and forth she would go, completely out of balance. Before long, she was tired and cranky all the time.

Are you like Amy? Do you go back and forth in your behaviors? Do you feel great one day and not-so-great the next? If so, chances are pretty good your pendulum is swinging back and forth in an unhealthy way. Take a look at your activities and your choices. Make sure everything is in balance. You want to spend more time on the balance beam, after all!

Why is it so important for girls who love Jesus to live balanced lives? For one thing, you need to stay healthy. Unbalanced girls end up with all sorts of issues like poor eating habits and lack of sleep. These can lead to stress, and stress can lead to sickness. Once their health is affected, girls who've lost their balance often struggle with their emotions, going back and forth between anger and tears.

Don't learn the hard way. Rest when you need to rest. Play when you need to play. Work when you need to work. And above all, spend time with the Lord. Seek Him daily. Dig into His Word to discover His perspective on your activities. Ask Him to restore balance to your life.

Balance, sweet girl. It's far more than walking a tightrope or staying up on a balance beam!

you can Learn to Be kinder

So, as those who have been chosen of God,
holy and beloved, put on a heart of compassion,
kindness, humility, gentleness and patience.
COLOSSIANS 3:12 NASB

Here's an interesting question: Can children be taught kindness? Is it something people can learn, like a lesson in school? Or are some people just going to go on being unkind forever?

Think of that boy who's always so mean. Maybe he lives in a home with no kindness at all. Maybe all he hears from his family is shouting. Maybe he's never encouraged, never bragged about, never given pats on the back. Because he has a hard home life, he has become mean toward others.

Can a boy like this grow up to be kind? Yes, he can! With the help of loving people like you, your teacher, and his friends, he can grow to be a kindhearted boy. It might take a while, but don't give up. Keep showing him kindness. You could make a huge difference in his life.

Jesus wants us to be kind. Why? Because you are a reflection of Him, and He is kind. He also knows that kindness wins people over. You never know! Those mean kids might be watching you right now and asking, "What's so different about her? Why is she always smiling?" You can be a good teacher.

Of course the best teacher is Jesus Himself. He looked on others with such kindness and compassion in His heart. We learn in His Word how to treat others. It's not always easy to show kindness, but it's always the best choice.

Take Janetta's story, for instance. A certain girl on her softball team made her a little crazy. She was a rough kid. This girl had a lot of attitude and rarely treated others well. Still, Janetta made up her mind to treat her kindly. The other kids on the team weren't so willing, but Janetta never gave up. She spent quality time with her, asked about her schoolwork, helped her with homework, and even offered to help with her pitching skills. Before long, the girl's heart softened. Wonder of wonders. . .she became nicer! The other kids noticed and responded. Before long, the entire team was different. This kindness eventually spilled over onto the girl's family, and multiple lives were changed, all because one girl decided to take the time to speak kindly.

Is there someone in your life like the girl in Janetta's story? We all know people who are difficult. They're not fun to be around. We have a hard time playing nice around them. Oh, but it's so worth it! Maybe you won't see the fruit of your kindness right away, but the payoff will come sooner or later.

How can you show kindness? Have a sweet way of talking. Be concerned when others are upset. Do random acts of kindness when people least expect it. Pray and ask the Lord what you can do. Most of all, learn to love the unlovable. It's worth it. *They* are worth it. After all, they are God's kids too.

You've Got Style

But [be] hospitable, a lover of good,
self-controlled, upright, holy, and disciplined.
TITUS 1:8 ESV

Marci was a girl with a lot of style. Her hair always looked great. She knew how to pick out the right clothes, right down to the perfect earrings and bracelets. Even her shoes matched her outfits. Friends always commented on how nice she looked. This "style" spilled over into the way she treated others. She was known for being kind and treating the kids at school with grace—even the tough kids.

If you looked past the stylish clothes and perfect hair, you might notice that Marci was a little overweight and had not-so-perfect teeth. But people didn't really pay attention to those things. They saw the real Marci, and to them, she was gorgeous every time because of her great attitude.

We all have a certain style about us, don't we? We have our own way of doing things. People know us at a glance because of our style. Whether we're casual or fancy, quirky or fun, we're all styling. And as with Marci, our style spills over into our attitudes and behaviors.

So what's your style? When people look at you, what do they think? When people look at some girls, they might say, "Wow, she looks like a girl who's a lot of fun! I'd like to get to know her!" For others they might say, "Wow, her family must really have money. Look at those expensive shoes she's wearing." For others the line might be, "Wow. Don't get close to that one. She looks scary!" This "first response" might seem a little judgmental, but let's face it—we all pay attention to others' style, whether we mean to or not.

What does style have to do with our spiritual walk? Quite a bit, if you think about it. We're not expected to put on a fashion show, so that's not the point. But we are representing Christ, so we don't want to turn up in public looking like a hot mess. Well, not all the time, anyway. But more importantly, we want our heart to shine through. Our "heart style" shouldn't turn people away but rather should draw them to us. And isn't that the point?

Jesus had His own style too. He wasn't handsome (according to the Bible), but people flocked to His side. Their attraction to Him had nothing to do with His clothing, to be sure. It had everything to do with His compassion and love for others. His "style show" went far beyond the physical and served as an invitation to others to draw near, to sit at His feet and learn. To love and be loved.

Let's follow the example of Christ today, girl. Put on a style show like His, then watch as others are drawn to you.

You Are a Daughter of the King

The King's daughter is all glorious within;
her clothing is interwoven with gold.
PSALM 45:13 NASB

Don't you love today's scripture? What a beautiful image of you, the daughter of the King, dressed in golden clothing. Wow! Nothing but the finest for a child of the King—that's what you are, after all!

It's perfectly normal for God's girls to want to be princesses, to dress in fancy gowns, and to live the life of royalty. You've probably been practicing since you were little. Think about it. Didn't you love to play dress-up when you were younger? You could hardly wait to open the box of costumes and reach inside. Which dress would you choose this time? The blue one? The pink? The yellow?

Every little girl enjoys looking like a princess. She can't wait to put on the flowing gown. The tiara. The jewels. She imagines what her life would be like in the castle. (A fun thing to imagine, right?)

As a princess, you want to skip from room to room in your Father's gorgeous house and greet your guests. Most of all you want to please your Daddy's heart. Nothing makes you happier than seeing the smile on the King's face as He looks adoringly at you. You want to dance for Him, to watch His eyes twinkle and His lips curl up in a delighted smile. Oh, how beautiful you feel when you spend time with the King. How loved!

This is more than just a fairy tale, girl! You really are a daughter of the King of Kings. You're royalty! And He adores you. Romans 8:14–17 says that you've been adopted by God. His Spirit makes you a daughter of the Most High God. As a result, you can call Him "Abba (Daddy) Father." You are His heir. Wow! That means you get to inherit all that your Father has available for you.

Today, pause to think about your life as a royal daughter of the King, then spend more time in His presence. Run to His throne. Settle in at His feet and ask Him what it means to be a daughter of the King. You are precious in His sight. More precious than all the jewels in the kingdom. So enjoy your life as a princess. It's who you were meant to be!

you will overcome

Do not be overcome by evil,
but overcome evil with good.
ROMANS 12:21 NASB

You are an overcomer!

Maybe you've read that in the Bible but you don't know what it means. If you break down the word *overcome*, it means to "come over" a situation, to move from one place to another. The problems you face sometimes feel like giant walls, don't they? You have to get from one side to the other. To overcome means you "come over" the wall that divides the two. You make the leap, never to go back.

How do you cross from one side to the other? It's kind of like that game you sometimes play: "Red Rover, Red Rover, let so-and-so come over." Remember how the game goes? You stand hand in hand with your teammates. Then when your name is called, you break free from the group and race across the open field to the opposite side. There's something about the cheers from your team members that gives you the courage to let go and run, run, run. You feel sure you can break through the barrier of the other team's linked arms! So you crash through...to victory! Wow—what energy! How strong you are. You're an overcomer!

The same is true in your life as a Christian. The book of Hebrews (chapter 12) says a great cloud of witnesses are watching you as you run your race as a believer. Think of them as your Red Rover friends, standing hand in hand. They want you to break through. They want you to overcome. Whenever you need encouragement, just read their stories: Read the story of Moses, who led his people to the Promised Land. Discover more about the life of Noah, who faced his fear and did what God commanded, though it made no sense at the time. Learn from Esther, who took a stand for her people and saved a nation. Think about the story of Jonah, who learned the hard way that you need to do what God says. Learn from young Timothy, who recognized God's gifts in his life. Discover the heart of an overcomer in young David, who faced the mighty Goliath with nothing but a slingshot and a few stones.

With the help of these very real people, you can learn how to get from one side of the obstacle to the other. Red Rover, Red Rover. . .you are an overcomer!

You Will Make Mistakes

*My dear children, I write this to you so that you will
not sin. But if anybody does sin, we have an advocate
with the Father—Jesus Christ, the Righteous One.*
1 JOHN 2:1 NIV

Have you figured out yet that you're not perfect? It's sad but true. You have good intentions (you mean to do the right thing), but sometimes you mess up. You are human, after all.

Take a look at the following sentences and fill in the blanks.

Remember that time I promised to clean my room, but instead I _____.

I'm embarrassed about that time at school when I _____
_____.

Sometimes when my friends start gossiping, I _____
_____.

When I talk back to my mom, I feel _____
_____.

I didn't mean to lie, but one time I said _____
_____.

If you're being completely honest, you have to admit. . .you've made mistakes. And you'll make even more as you grow older. All people do. You'll never be perfect until you get to heaven.

Here's some amazing news. When you mess up, you have Someone who can help fix things. The Bible says that Jesus (your Savior) is like a lawyer in a courtroom. You mess up and He goes to the judge and says, "Your Honor, this girl blew it! She really messed up this time. She admits it, and she feels bad."

The judge says, "I see. There will have to be a punishment, of course."

Then Jesus (your lawyer) says, "Judge, I have decided to take her punishment so that she can go free."

Wow! Now that's some lawyer. Jesus stands in the gap for you. He takes the penalty for you. He talks to the judge (God) for you. All you have to do is tell Him that you're sorry and that you want to live for Him.

If you're feeling guilty today for the many times you've done wrong things, it's not too late to turn things around. You can pray this simple prayer: "Jesus, I'm sorry for what I've done. I want to do better. Can You help me? Please come and live in my heart, Jesus. Be the Lord of my life. I want to live for You from this moment on! Amen."

When you pray that prayer, everything can change in an instant. Jesus becomes your lawyer, and your case is dismissed!

Your Dreams Can Be Supersized

And the LORD answered me: "Write the vision; make it plain on tablets, so he may run who reads it. For still the vision awaits its appointed time; it hastens to the end—it will not lie. If it seems slow, wait for it; it will surely come; it will not delay."
HABAKKUK 2:2–3 ESV

If you've ever been to a fast food restaurant, you know they always seem to ask the same question when you order a burger, fries, and a drink: "Would you like to supersize that?" To supersize the meal means they give you a jumbo-sized drink and enough fries for an army! Most of the time Mom says, "No!" For one thing, that's a lot of food! For another, supersizing can get expensive. (And who really needs that much soda, anyway? Talk about a sugar rush!)

Meals might not be a great thing to supersize, but when it comes to your faith, God is all about going big! He wants to take your dreams (who you want to be when you grow up, where you want to go, what you want to do) and supersize them. He wants you to dream bigger. He wants you to go further, to make a real difference for Him. No small dreams for you! God has big stuff in your future.

Look at today's Bible verse. God tells Habakkuk to write down his vision and to make it plain. He was asking

Habakkuk to make a plan and stick with it. Have you ever had to do that? Maybe you have a big project coming up and you need to make a to-do list so that you get everything done in time. Maybe you're throwing a party and you have decorations to buy, food to prepare, guests to invite. Will you ever be ready in time if you don't prepare? You make your list and check it twice. You mark things off one by one until the day of the party arrives and everything is done.

God wants you to be prepared for your grown-up life. So start now by writing down the things the Lord is telling you. When He gives you ideas for your future, write them down in a safe place. (When you're an adult, you can go back and read them. It will be a lot of fun!)

Supersize your dreams, girl. Let your imagination soar. Trust God with the details. He's got this!

YOU ARE BEAUTIFUL

*Do not let your adorning be external—the braiding of
hair and the putting on of gold jewelry, or the clothing
you wear—but let your adorning be the hidden person
of the heart with the imperishable beauty of a gentle
and quiet spirit, which in God's sight is very precious.*
1 PETER 3:3–4 ESV

You're a beautiful girl. Oh, sure. . .you don't always feel
beautiful, but you are. What makes you so lovely isn't just
what people can see with their eyes, but how you make
them feel in their hearts. In other words, you're gorgeous
from the inside out.

Think about this for a minute: A lot of girls (even grown
women) don't like the way they look. They work extra hard
to make themselves look beautiful with makeup and pretty
clothes. There's nothing wrong with wanting to look lovely
on the outside, but what if you went to all that trouble but
never fixed your bad attitude or the snippy way you spoke
to others?

For example, what would be the point of putting on
lovely eye makeup yet not paying attention to the things
your eyes look at? What would be the point of putting on
lipstick and then using our mouth to speak ugly things to or

about people? What would be the point of using concealer to cover blemishes on your skin but then deliberately hurting others with your actions?

Rebecca had a hard time figuring this out. She worked on her external appearance. . .a lot. Not that she needed to. She was already a natural beauty. People everywhere said so. But sometimes the inside didn't match the outside. Her words were harsh. Her attitude was cold. She wondered why people walked to the other side of the room whenever she would come around. Wasn't she drawing them in with her beauty? Obviously not. It took a while for her to figure it out, but eventually she understood what needed to change and cleaned up her attitude so that the internal matched the external.

There's nothing we can do to the outward body to make the internal soul look pretty to others. Only our love, our kindness, and our heartfelt compassion will beautify us from the inside out. And those things—like every good thing—come from the Father above.

You Are a Girl Who Loves

*And so we know and rely on the love
God has for us. God is love. Whoever
lives in love lives in God, and God in them.*
1 JOHN 4:16 NIV

God placed an amazing love in your heart for people. You don't know how to explain it, but you feel deeply for those you meet. That girl at the bus stop who stands by herself. You love her and pray for her all the time. You do your best to make her feel like she has a friend. That older lady at church, the one who always sits by herself. You stop by and give her a hug every Sunday because you want her to know that someone adores her.

It's so easy to make people feel loved. Here are a few things you can do: Send a little note to someone who lives in a nursing home. Let them know they are not forgotten. Send a care package to a missionary in a foreign country. He needs to be reminded that someone back home is thinking of him. Pick up the phone and call your favorite aunt. Tell her how special she is to you and that you've been thinking of her. Save your money to buy Mom a necklace with a little heart on it. That way she can wear it and be reminded that you love her.

God loves when you love others. He created you to do that. That's why it comes so naturally to you—He planted that love-seed deep in your heart.

Of course, not everyone is so lovable. That mean boy who picks on you? God wants you to love him too. That lady who always seems to have her face puckered up like she's been eating sour candy? Be sweet to her too. She's probably going through struggles you know nothing about. That girl at school who seems like such a snob? If you knew what she was really going through at home, you'd probably understand why she acts that way.

Love everyone—no matter how they act or dress or what they look like. Love everyone, because that's what Jesus did, and you want to be like Him.

YOU MAKE A DIFFERENCE

*"For God did not send his Son into the world to condemn
the world, but to save the world through him."*
JOHN 3:17 NIV

Mary watched as an artist worked on a new painting. For the first few minutes she couldn't make any sense of his color choices. It looked a little strange. Then as he added just a little bit of brown to the top of the canvas, she realized. . .he was painting a man's face. After that, everything else made sense.

Sometimes life is like that. We can't make any sense out of where things are heading. We wonder if the road is going forward at all. Then, suddenly, we get it.

So many people in this world feel stuck. They can't seem to get past where they are right here, right now. Life's circumstances have them frozen in place. These people are all around us. The woman at the grocery store. The child on the bicycle. The man in the business suit. That girl sitting next to you in class. That boy on the playground. They might look perfectly normal on the outside, but on the inside many feel disappointed, like a painting with no color. Their lives aren't turning out the way they'd hoped.

What does this have to do with being a difference maker? Everything. You can be that splash of color that brings sense to a senseless picture. You can give a word of encouragement to set them free. You can offer hope when they're feeling hopeless. You might say, "I'm just a kid! I can't do that." Oh, but you can.

Here's an example: Mary met a lady who lived on her street, a single mother with six children. They had no food in their house. Mary talked to the pastor at her church and asked if she could have some food from the church's food pantry. The pastor said yes. Before long, the mother and children were in a much better place, and not just their bellies. They soon started coming to church and gave their hearts to the Lord. One of the daughters joined the worship team. She became a worship leader, all because one person took the time to share some food with them. That little splash of color from Mary brought the whole picture into focus for the mother and six children.

Difference makers aren't looking after their own happiness. They have real compassion for others. They put action to their words and produce fruit in their lives. Instead of saying, "I wonder how I can get more out of this day," they say, "I wonder how I can make this day better for someone else." Then they pray that God will send into their path people who need a special touch.

Who are you going to touch today? What splashes of color will you add to a friend's (or stranger's) life?

You Celebrate God's Plans

"For I know the plans I have for you,"
says the LORD. "They are plans for good and
not for disaster, to give you a future and a hope."
JEREMIAH 29:11 NLT

Have you ever noticed that God's plans don't always match up with our own? We're so good at setting things in motion—and many of us are equally good at carrying through—but what happens when we get ahead of God? Have you ever done that?

Misty did. She often came up with terrific God-like ideas. They were very spiritual, in fact. Some of them included teaching a Bible study before school, collecting food for the homeless, working at a shelter on the holidays, and much more. On and on the list went, and all of it to share God's love with others. Lives were changed. People were blessed.

Good stuff, right? Only, the timing wasn't always right. And her parents weren't always thrilled with her ideas. Sometimes she did these things, not because she'd prayed about them and had God's stamp of approval, but because they just "seemed" like the right things to do.

Stop to think about that. Maybe you're just as busy as

Misty. You have amazing ideas (or so you think). Have you ever put the cart ahead of the horse? Ever stepped out on the road without God's say-so? If so, then you know that "oops!" feeling that can come along with it.

Sometimes you get so excited, so pumped with zeal and drive, that you forget to pray before you take action. And when you sense the call of God on your life to make a difference in the world, you have to be even more careful! You're likely to do every project that "feels" right, simply because you see the good in it.

And there is good in it! So much good, in fact, that someone else might get some benefit out of heading it up. Did you ever think about that? If you step back, someone else might get a chance to be blessed by taking on the project. Sure, you won't have the satisfaction of saying, "I did that!" but do you really need to?

Prayer. Slow decisions. Accountability partners. These are all good things, girl! They keep you in balance. Staying in balance frees you up to do the things that God has truly called you to do, things that can make you soar! So take your time. Don't jump in headfirst. Seek God first and then take a deep breath. . .and wait. His plans for your life are perfect. Yours? Not so much.

Home is where the Heart is

*The wise woman builds her house, but with her
own hands the foolish one tears hers down.*
PROVERBS 14:1 NIV

Hanging out with friends at school is so much fun. And you love, love, love going to the park or the pool to play or swim. You have a blast on vacations, visiting the ocean or the mountains. And isn't it awesome to go to great places like museums and art galleries? You would be a world traveler if you could!

Yes, you love to see new places, but the very best place to be—the place you love most of all—is your home. Why do you suppose you love your home so much? Is it because it's familiar? Probably! After all, you know what each room looks like. You know that the yellow pillows are on the brown sofa and the green pillows are on the love seat. You know how you feel when you walk into your bedroom at night, cozy and comfy.

Maybe you love your home because the people you love are there. You know that Mom (or Dad) will tuck you in at night and tell you they love you. Your sister (or brother) will be right down the hall in the other bedroom. You feel safe whenever they're all around.

Your house is so special. Every piece of furniture, each photo on the wall, even the dishes in the kitchen—they all make you feel at home. You love how the sunlight beams in through the blinds in the morning, and you enjoy peering out that same window each night to see the moon. You like sitting on the sofa watching movies with your family. You have a blast playing hide-and-seek in the backyard with your friends. You love everything about your home.

God gave you that home as a safe place to live and grow. It doesn't matter if you live in a mansion or a tiny apartment. God doesn't care if you have a room of your own or share a room with a couple of sisters. He has given you a special place to live where you can be yourself.

He has another home for you too! One day you'll live in heaven. There you'll have a mansion. The streets will be made of gold. You'll know nothing but love in this awesome place. All the people who love God will be your neighbors. You'll be one big happy family, worshipping Him forever and ever. It will be the most amazing home ever. Until then, go ahead and thank God for the special place He has given you to live right here, right now.

You Love God's Word

For the word of God is alive and active. Sharper than any double-edged sword, it penetrates even to dividing soul and spirit, joints and marrow; it judges the thoughts and attitudes of the heart.
HEBREWS 4:12 NIV

If you're a strong reader, a true book lover, you find it hard to put a good story down. You'll try to get by with reading "just a chapter" before bed but find yourself turning the page to the next chapter, then the next. The story captivates you, draws you in.

The Bible is loaded with life-changing stories that will keep you on the edge of your seat. True swashbuckling heroes fighting formidable foes. Damsels in distress. Men of valor. Women of courage. The stories weave in and out in a lovely array, drawing you in and speaking a beautiful message of faith. You can learn so much from the characters in these stories. Bible stories are better than any novel you will ever read because these heroes really existed. They walked on this earth and faced many of the same challenges that you face.

Have you paused to think that through? Moses was very real. So was Abraham. And Elijah. And David. And Deborah.

All the great difference makers were real men and women who truly loved the Lord and lived to serve Him. Their stories are more than just tales of good and evil; they're real pictures of people—like you—who faced battles head-on and won.

Do you ever wonder if these great men and women realized their stories would be passed down? Did they have any idea that thousands of years later, people would still learn from their life lessons? It's fascinating to consider how the story of God's people has carried on, well past Bible times into the present. And you're part of that story. If the great writers from those days were still writing down stories of faith, yours would slide right in alongside the others. People could read it hundreds or even thousands of years from now.

When you see the Bible as more than just a storybook—when you read about the life and ministry of Jesus and His journey to the cross—you can't help but stand in awe that this marvelous Word has stood the test of time and is ours even today. It is, by far, the most valuable book you will ever read, loaded with answers for every question, examples for every life challenge, and wisdom for every decision. No wonder you love it so much, sweet girl! In it, you find all you will ever need!

Well, what are you waiting for? Go grab your Bible and dive in! There are heroes of the faith just waiting for you to read their stories.

Your work matters

Anything I wanted, I would take. I denied myself
no pleasure. I even found great pleasure in
hard work, a reward for all my labors.
ECCLESIASTES 2:10 NLT

Would the people who know you best say that you're a hard worker? Do you do your tasks with energy and joy? It's easy to spot the people who love their work. It shows on their faces. What is your face showing as you work, work, work?

God loves a hard worker, and you want to please Him, but sometimes you slack off. You wonder if the things you're doing are making a difference. You work, work, work on a school paper, but who's going to remember it fifty years from now? You slave away organizing your room, but it just gets messy again. You make your bed in the morning, only to unmake it at night. Does it all really matter?

Here's the truth: your work does matter! It matters to God, of course. He wants you to be responsible in all areas of your life. He's training you to do great things for His kingdom when you're grown. It matters to your parents. They're watching closely to make sure you do the things you say you'll do. They are trying to raise you to be strong and independent. It matters to your teachers. They are watching you learn more each passing day because they want you to do well in school. It matters to your friends. Whether you realize it or not, they're watching the things you do. Most of all, though, it matters to you. The person who benefits the most from your hard work is you!

How do you benefit, you ask? The harder you work, the stronger your spiritual muscles become. You're like a weight lifter. The more you practice, the more you can lift. Over time, you'll be able to accomplish great things for God if you don't give up now.

Oh, I know. . .it's hard to keep going sometimes. You get tired. But remember, Jesus never gave up. He worked hard to pay for your salvation. Follow His example. Give every task your best effort. No slacking off!

you Are constant in prayer

Be joyful in hope, patient in affliction, faithful in prayer.
ROMANS 12:12 NIV

At the beginning of the new year, Julie had every intention of reading her Bible every day and praying at a specific time. She did well for the first week or so but then started slipping. Having a set time to read and pray didn't always work out for her, and she often ended up feeling guilty if she missed out.

Maybe you're like Julie. You've tried to get in the routine of reading and praying at the same time every day. For a lot of girls, this plan works great. Others have a harder time sticking to a set schedule. It's a great idea to try to read a certain number of chapters per day or pray for a set length of time, but what's really important is spending time with Him. It's your heart He's after, not a certain number of minutes.

Imagine you have a really good friend, one you talk with every day. She's your go-to person whenever you have a problem. The two of you share pretty much everything. Then one day her mom gets a new job and her family moves to another state. You still "see" each other on social media and occasionally speak by phone, but things just aren't the same. You would miss her, right? Most of all, you would miss your heart-to-heart conversations and the comfort you felt knowing you had someone you could turn to.

Now think about your prayer life. God is the ultimate Friend we can turn to when we're needing someone to listen. Those treasured conversations you're missing with your friend? The Lord is hoping you'll want to share them with Him. That's what prayer is—a sweet one-on-one conversation with Someone you love. And who loves you more than the One who created you?

So stop thinking about prayer as a "have to" thing. It was never meant to be a pain or a struggle. It's a precious conversation with Someone you adore. It's a lengthy pour-out-your-heart chat. It's a quick, rushed "Please, Lord, protect me!" It's a quiet "Thank You for Your blessings, Father," followed by a list of things you're most grateful for. It's a tearful "I don't get it, Lord" when things are falling apart and a "Praise the Lord! Hallelujah!" when all is going well.

Prayer is a day-in-and-day-out conversation with God. He doesn't care if you meet with Him at 6:00 a.m. or at noon. He doesn't care if you chat for an hour or for three minutes. What matters to Him is the desire to come to Him with all of your cares, concerns, joys, and sorrows. He will meet you there and wipe away every tear.

You Speak Life

*The Spirit alone gives eternal life. Human effort
accomplishes nothing. And the very words I
have spoken to you are spirit and life.*
JOHN 6:63 NLT

Your words matter. What you say—to others and to yourself—is very important. Don't believe it? Just ask Callie.
She got really bummed because she made a bad grade on a
math test. She started saying things like, "I'm just so stupid,"
and "I can't do this. I'm terrible at math. I'm such a loser."

Those words stuck to her, and before long she was really
struggling in class. Finally, her teacher had a long talk with
her. She explained that Callie was a good student. She just
needed to start seeing herself that way.

From that day on, Callie started saying things like, "I
can do this! I can do all things through Christ who gives me
strength!" She began to see an improvement in her attitude
and in her grades. Best of all, she felt better, not just about
herself, but about everything. And people noticed the change
in her. Instead of frowning all the time, she now had a smile
on her face. Others were encouraged just being around her.

Have you ever been like Callie? Do you catch yourself
saying things like, "I'm such a loser," or "I'll never be able to

do what other kids can do"? Those words are powerful. They plant themselves in your brain and your heart, and before long you start to believe them.

It's time to change what you say about yourself. The Bible says that you should build yourself up in your most holy faith. So don't focus on what you can't do. Instead, focus on what God can and will do through you! Make this your new motto: "I'm a child of the King! He can do great things through me!"

Here are some great verses to memorize. Say them out loud, speaking life over your situations:

- But thank God! He gives us victory over sin and death through our Lord Jesus Christ. (1 Corinthians 15:57 NLT)
- For we are God's masterpiece. He has created us anew in Christ Jesus, so we can do the good things he planned for us long ago. (Ephesians 2:10 NLT)
- "For I know the plans I have for you," says the LORD. "They are plans for good and not for disaster, to give you a future and a hope." (Jeremiah 29:11 NLT)
- "Those who are victorious will sit with me on my throne, just as I was victorious and sat with my Father on his throne." (Revelation 3:21 NLT)

you believe in miracles

*I ask you again, does God give you the Holy Spirit
and work miracles among you because you obey
the law? Of course not! It is because you believe
the message you heard about Christ.*
GALATIANS 3:5 NLT

If someone asked, "Do you believe in miracles?" what would you say? Do you still believe that God performs miracles? Can He still heal the sick? Can He turn tragedies into blessings? Can He heal broken marriages—or broken bones?

So many verses in the Bible show that God still works miracles. Maybe you've already witnessed a few but don't realize it. Maybe someone you know was in a terrible accident and doctors didn't think she would make it. . .but she did. Maybe your grandfather got really sick and the doctors didn't expect him to pull through. . .but he did. Maybe your friend's mom and dad were going to get a divorce but then decided not to. God performed another miracle! He helped them work things out.

If anyone asks what you believe, be ready to tell them: "Jesus Christ is the same yesterday, today, and forever"(Hebrews 13:8 NLT). If He performed miracles long ago (and He did), then you can be sure He will perform them now. Our wonderful Creator *never* changes. That's a promise from His Word.

Still not convinced? Sometimes miracles happen right in front of us and we don't even notice. Your body is performing miracles even now! If you were exposed to germs today (and you were), your immune system is hard at work, fighting them off. That cut on your finger? That scrape on your knee? Your miraculous body is healing those areas on its own. Your own body is a living, breathing miracle!

If you ever start to doubt, just remember these scriptures:

- I will meditate on your majestic, glorious splendor and your wonderful miracles. (Psalm 145:5 NLT)
- When he reached the place where the road started down the Mount of Olives, all of his followers began to shout and sing as they walked along, praising God for all the wonderful miracles they had seen. (Luke 19:37 NLT)

Yes, God still works miracles. He won't ever stop because there will always be people who need them. He can turn even the hardest heart back to Him. Don't stop praying for that one person who bugs you the most. Just trust that God, who never changes, can do wondrous things!

your Best Days Are Ahead

There are many who say, "Who will show us some good?
Lift up the light of your face upon us, O LORD!"
PSALM 4:6 ESV

Think back over the best days you've ever had in your life.
In fact, it might be fun to make a list. What was your favorite holiday get-together? Was it that Christmas when
you got the bike? What was your favorite trip you took with
your family? Was it the one where you went to the Grand
Canyon? What was the best church camp you ever went to,
the best birthday party you ever attended, the best slumber party you ever went to? Chances are pretty good you
had a blast at all of them!

You've had a lot of good days in your life, probably
even more than you can remember. There were days when
you had sweet conversations with people you love (like
close friends and grandparents). There were days when you
ate amazing, yummy food and your tummy felt so full you
thought you would pop. There were days when you laughed
until you cried. What fun you had on those special days.

Your list is probably getting longer now, isn't it? Have
you included the time you got a really good grade on that
test? What about the time you performed in the school play

and everyone told you how great you were? What about your summer trips to the pool or the lake? And how about that time you got to go on a boat with your best friend's family? You've had some amazing adventures, girl.

Are you starting to see that your life has been filled with hundreds and hundreds of remarkable days? If you take the time to think about it, you'll see that you have much to be grateful for. If each day represented one page in a book, it would be a very thick book!

God has given you a wonderful life with countless adventures. Isn't it wonderful of Him to fill your life with amazing people to share those adventures with? You have parents, grandparents, aunts, uncles, cousins, friends, and so many more. They make your life even more exciting.

Here's some really fun news: your best days are ahead of you. It's true! There are so many adventures you haven't even gone on yet! There are trips you'll take, people you'll meet, worship experiences you'll have. . .and each one will be a big surprise when it comes. Don't ever forget that God knows the number of your days and wants you to have an amazing time celebrating every moment.

your Job Isn't Finished

*Keep his decrees and commands, which I am giving
you today, so that it may go well with you and your
children after you and that you may live long in the
land the LORD your God gives you for all time.*
DEUTERONOMY 4:40 NIV

Remember that time you started a puzzle but gave up about halfway through? And what about that time when you started a craft project but didn't finish it?

Nothing half done is ever pretty to look at. A half-clean room isn't clean. A half-washed car isn't truly washed. A half-baked cake is just plain icky. A half-done job isn't done at all.

God wants you to be a girl who finishes what she starts. You need to have a good attitude to be a finisher. Let's say you have a big project due for school. You have two weeks to complete it. You start out with a bang. It's going to be great. Then you give up about halfway into it. The night before it's due, you try to pull it together, but it's just not turning out the way you'd hoped. You feel like giving up, but that's not possible, so you slap it together and try to make it work.

The next day you take your project to school, and you're embarrassed when you see how much better all the others look. You wish you'd spent more time on it so that you could have finished well. Finishing poorly has left you feeling bad, so you promise yourself you'll do better next time.

The same is true in your spiritual life. Remember that friend you've been praying for? Don't stop praying, even if she treats you badly. Keep on with what you started. Remember how you said you were going to witness to your friends? You said you would tell them about Jesus. You started to but then got scared. Don't give up! They need to know about His saving love.

So many areas of your life need a strong finish. Remember how you started cleaning out your closet but got overwhelmed? Get back in there! Finish what you started. Remember how you promised yourself you would eat healthier? Don't give up now! The race isn't over until you cross the finish line. There's still a lot of work to be done.

Be a girl who finishes well every time. You'll be so glad you did.

scripture index